Climb High Rocks State Park

Copyright 2010 Paul Nick

ISBN 978-0-557-72152-8

ACKNOWLEDGMENTS

This guidebook could not have been completed without the direct or indirect assistance of the following people: Michael Flood, Jeff Gagliano, Mark Ronca, Neil J.A. Sloane and also Warren Musselman and Tom Stryker, the authors of the 1985 guidebook, *Red Rock: A Climber's Guide To High Rocks*.

DEDICATION

This book is dedicated to the staff of The Access Fund, working tirelessly on behalf of climbers to keep our crags open to climbing. If you are not a member yet, please go to www.accessfund.org now and join up. This is the easiest and one of the best ways to give something back to rock climbing.

Front Cover Photo: Climbers on Tango

Back Cover Photo: Jeff Gagliano on Wild Wall

"Neil Sloane on Hummingbird"

CONTENTS:

Warning and Disclaimer 1
Introduction 3
The Descent Trail 13
The Practice Face 15
The Neolithic Wall 16
The Tango Wall 22
The Weeping Wall 25
The Cramped Face 27
The Great Buttress 30
Open Face and Orangutan Buttress 37
Garden of Eden Buttress 42
Hawk's Nest Area 46
Noncensus Area 55
Joshua Wall 58
Chain Reaction Buttress 60
Obnoxious Partner Buttress 64
Phone Booth Buttress 66
Grey Rocks 71
Red Rocks Remote 75
Index 79

WARNING AND DISCLAIMER

Any form of rock climbing or bouldering is dangerous, and you could be seriously injured or die. Neither the author nor publisher can assure the accuracy of any information contained in this guide book. This includes, but is not limited to route grades, protection ratings, descriptions, location of fixed protection, route lines on photos, etc. Even if the information was accurate at the time of writing, the cliffs at High Rocks are known to change over time due to vegetation, freeze thaw cycles, etc. This guide book is definitely not an instruction manual for climbing.

Do not depend on this in any form or fashion book for your safety. You must rely on your own judgment at all times, and if there is any question about your judgment, seek a professional guide or instructor. Do not trust any fixed protection. If you are not certain that you can complete a climb without endangering yourself or others, DO NOT PROCEED. There is a very long tradition of self-reliance in the sport of rock climbing, and the responsibility for any accidents is yours only.

INTRODUCTION

The popular shale and argillite cliffs located within High Rocks State Park, near Point Pleasant, Pennsylvania, have been referred to by a variety of names including High Rocks, Red Rocks, Boileau Rocks, Ralph Stover, and oftentimes simply "Stover". Note that Ralph Stover State Park is nearby, but the cliffs are technically in High Rocks State Park.

The shale cliffs overlook the scenic Tohickon Gorge which can be viewed from various overlooks along the cliff top trail. The stream at the bottom of the gorge attracts rafters and kayakers at certain times of the year when the dam floodgates are opened upstream.

The main cliffs at High Rocks vary between 40 and 100 feet in height. Most of the routes have a single pitch of climbing that can be top-roped if desired. For beginners, High Rocks is a superb area because top-ropes can be easily anchored on most of the easier climbs. For traditional lead climbers, there is a nice collection of strenuous but reasonably protected routes up to 5.10a in difficulty, some with two pitches of climbing. Lead-able routes harder than 5.8 are mostly bolted. For advanced climbers, there are a handful of 5.12 routes and some boulder problems in the V4 to V8 range.

Routes at High Rocks typically surmount one or more strenuous overhangs. The rock is unusual in that most holds are smooth lips or plates. Since climbing on many different types of rock is important for developing climbing technique, the unusual rock here can contribute to the diversity of your climbing experience.

High Rocks is a great place to climb on a sunny winter day when the temperature is still within reason. The cliffs block most of the wind and the sun beats directly upon the rock. As a result, it is not unusual for the base of the cliff to feel tens of degrees warmer than the parking lot and for the rock to feel toastier than the surrounding air.

Geography: Two types of rock are encountered when climbing at High Rocks:

- **Brunswick Shale:** Friable, crumbly rock that can rattle your nerves if you are leading. This type of rock is encountered on such routes as Dean's List and the Phone Booth.

- **Lockatong Argillite:** Smoother, harder and denser than Brunswick Shale. Often forms smooth faces and sharp corners, ledges and overhangs. The Tango route and the lower half of the Practice Face are on this type of rock.

Access Issues: Although climbing is accepted by the park, there is concern about the strain placed upon the environment by the large number of visitors (including non-climbers such as mountain-bikers). Occasionally there have been accidents that could have been avoided if standard safety precautions had been followed: always double-check your knots and harness, always stay tied in when on ledges, do not push yourself on lead unless your protection is bomb-proof and make sure every component of a top-rope anchor is redundant.

Ethics: The general consensus among local climbers is as follows:

- Please do not throw down a rope from the top of the crag until you have yelled "ROPE" and have waited a minute or so for people to answer and get out of the way.

- Please remove trash left by less respectful visitors to the park. Minimal effort is needed to bend down and pick up a cigarette butt or candy wrapper. In recent years, cigarette butts have been accumulating at the base of popular routes which does not create a positive image of the climbing community.

- High Rocks is subject to severe erosion in places. Whenever possible, stick to the established trails and avoid disturbing areas of thin ground cover.

- Do not chop any trees or disturb the cactus plants that grow on some of the ledges.

- There is a Port-O-John in the parking lot. Please use it!

- Due to the nature of the rock, fixed gear has always been necessary for adequate protection on many routes. While replacing rusty or damaged pitons and bolts is acceptable, it is not okay to add additional fixed gear without reaching a consensus with local climbers. This is especially true of any routes that are historically important. When bolts need to be added or replaced, colored hangers are preferred. Metolius "Red Rock" EnviroHangers or the equivalent can significantly reduce the visual impact of bolts at High Rocks.

Hazards: In the event of an emergency, call 911. If you do not have a cell phone, there is a public emergency phone in the parking lot.

Beware of a virulent strain of poison ivy with leaves often of an extraordinary size. If you are highly allergic to poison ivy, avoid the area during the summer.

Beware of loose and friable rock. The rock is soft and changes somewhat every year because of freeze and thaw cycles. For example, a few years prior to the publishing of this book, a huge block fell from the Tango roof, changing the character of the routes there. If leading, pay close attention to the soundness of the rock around your protection.

Assume that all tree anchors are less sound than they appear. In particular, never rely on a single tree for an anchor. Soil compaction caused by the weight of many park visitors has been known to starve roots of water, causing them to rot beneath the surface.

Most of the original quarter-inch bolts have been replaced with safer 3/8 inch bolts. There may still be a few old pitons on some routes, and these should not be used at all.

The under-cliff trail is dangerously narrow in spots, with a potentially lethal drop-off. It may be best to leave young kids at home.

In the past, cars have occasionally been broken into, mostly on weekdays. Do not leave anything valuable in your car and avoid having it appear as a tempting target.

Climbing History: Much of the early history of the area was preserved in a well researched article, "The Climbing Cliffs of Stover", by John Guyer in the December 1965 issue of Appalachia magazine. Although High Rocks is a small crag, it has a long history that begins around 1750.

Circa 1750: Joseph and Moses Doan, local miscreants and fugitives from the law, ascended the cliffs via a gully to escape the retribution of the militia. Whether their act reflects the anti-establishment roots of climbing is uncertain. What is known is that they didn't get too far. Moses was shot dead even as Joseph kicked and dangled from a noose outside their cabin a few hundred yards upstream from the cliffs.

1930s and 40s: The central figure of these years is Joe Walsh. Walsh had learned to climb from a group that included Arnold Wexler whose essay "Belaying the Leader" strongly influenced the early evolution of American climbing technique. In the mid-1930s, Joe Walsh and other members of the Philadelphia Trail Club came upon the High Rocks cliffs during an afternoon hike. Walsh and other club members soon returned to establish the first technical rock climb in the area, a hundred-foot chimney known as *The Long Chimney* (5.3). Using a hemp rope and home-made pitons and carabiners, Walsh also made first ascents of *Ivy Leaf* (5.4), *The Airy Route* (5.3) and *Loose Block* (5.2). After World War II, Joe Walsh returned and climbed *Open Face* (5.5), *Three Buttresses* (5.5) and several others.

1950s: Around 1954, climbers from the Philadelphia Grotto of the National Speological Society and from local college outdoor clubs began to climb at High Rocks. In particular, George Austin and Roland Machold stand out for their first ascents of *Hawk's Nest* (5.6), *Rattlesnake* (5.7) and especially *Orangutan* (5.8, FA:1954) with its exciting and exposed "Crack of Doom" crux. This was the first 5.8 at High Rocks and one of the first in the Eastern U.S.

Lou Lutz and Bob Chambers began climbing at High Rocks with the University of Pennsylvania Outing Club. Their most notable ascents were *Gorilla* (5.6), *Director Overhang* (5.8) and *Zig Zag* (5.8). Bob Chambers, an Englishman studying physics at the University of Pennsylvania, spurned the use of pitons and climbed instead with runners, knotted slings, wedged pebbles and machine nuts. Although he was chided by fellow climbers for his eccentric style, he was far ahead of his time. In fact, it wasn't until the 1970s that "clean climbing" swept the country.

Also notable in this decade was the free ascent of *Neanderthal* (8+) in 1957. On the same day that Lou Lutz and Bob Chambers aided this route, M.G. Block and Gordon Dickson free climbed it, protecting themselves using the bolts just placed on the aid ascent (these can still be seen on the route). Neanderthal, with its intimidating and strenuous roof, was not repeated until 1963 and was considered a test-piece for many years afterwards.

1960s: It is interesting to note that at the end of 1957, three 5.8 routes existed at High Rocks while at the Shawangunks there were only two 5.8 routes - *Minnie Bell* and *Fat Stick*. After these high standards were set by the early pioneers, High Rocks began to stagnate and fell far behind other areas in the 1960's. Most climbers viewed High Rocks as a training area and were content to repeat existing routes. Hence, only a handful of new routes appeared in the 60's with none harder than 5.8.

1970s: After Peter Kolman and Kirby Ellis published the "Green Guide" in 1974, first ascent activity began to increase. In 1977, Bill Shaniman led and freed the aid climb *Crummy Rotten Crack*, the area's first 5.10. In 1979 Mel Hamel's and Tom Stryker's adventurous siege produced the classic Stover face climb, *Tales From The Crypt* (5.10a), which was later retro-bolted.

1980s: In the early 1980s, Tom Stryker, Tom Moffat and Mel Hamel established many additional 5.10 routes on increasingly poor quality rock. In 1984, Englishman Paul Craven visited High Rocks and lead (on sight) the area's classic overhanging top-rope problem, *Phone Booth* (10a X). Early in 1985, Colin Lanz's wild dynamic lunge on the Tango Roof produced *Mass X Energy = Swing*, the area's first 5.11 established on lead.

Many of the classic boulder problems were also put up in the 1980s, mostly by Mel Hamel, Tom Stryker and Colin Lanz. Colin Lanz, a particularly strong and talented climber, pushed the limits of roped climbing (Violent Femmes, 5.13), bouldering (Marty Broke It, V8) and personal boldness (Stand & Deliver, V5 R). Colin is said to have soloed the overhanging route, *Multiple Arrests, No Convictions* (10), in light rain with a cast on one leg!

1990s: With all the natural lines already climbed, most significant new routes in the 1990's were established as bolted sport climbs. For example, two routes were bolted and lead on the overhanging wall at the top of the Great Zawn gulley, namely *The Problem* (12a, FA: Dean Hernandez) and *Man Of Science* (12c/d, FA: Michael Flood).

In 1995, the Ralph Stover Climber's Coalition formed to address access and environmental impact issues. The R.S.C.C. established trails, replaced old bolts and anchors, performed trash clean-ups, erected an information kiosk and more. The Coalition has been presented with an award of merit by the Pennsylvania Department of Conservation and Natural Resources and has gained national praise from the Access Fund commending the quality and scope of the High Rocks newsletter. Unfortunately, the organization did not survive when its dedicated president, Mike Flood, moved onto other things.

"Logo for former Ralph Stover Climber's Coalition"

Climb High Rocks State Park 9

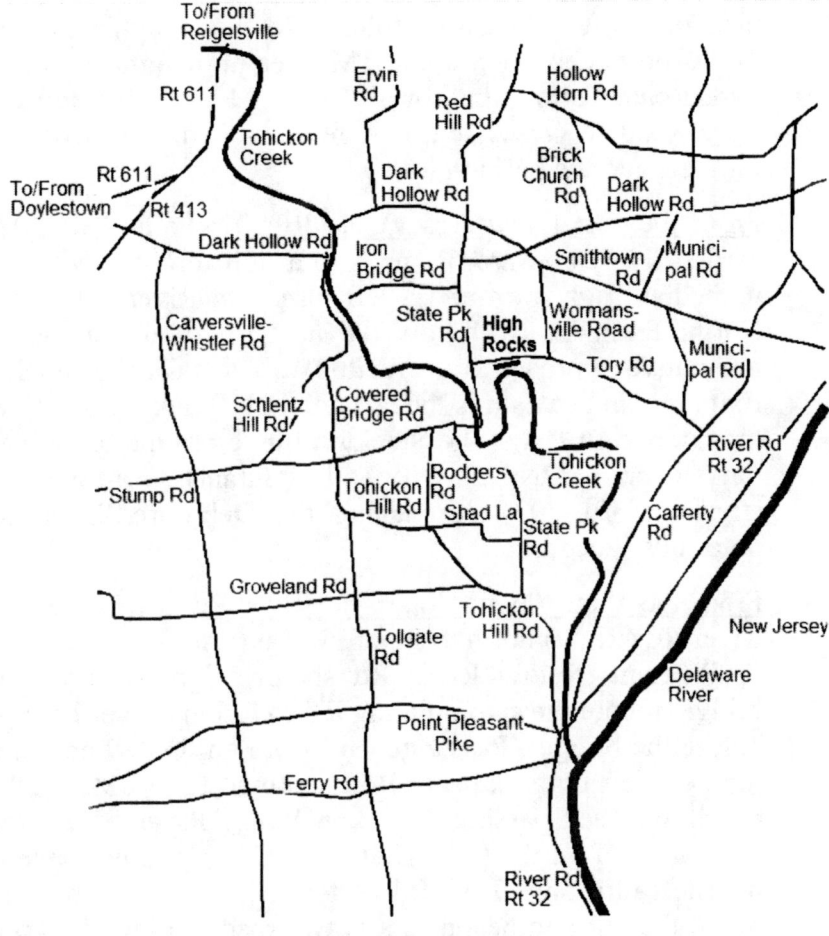

"Local Roadmap"

2000s: In 2005, a huge block fell from the Tango Roof eliminating a climb, but changing Gorilla from 5.7 to 5.11d. A few new sport climbs went up on the Non Census buttress, but generally the area is thoroughly developed.

Directions: High Rocks State Park is located along the Tohickon Creek, in Bucks County, Pennsylvania, not far from the Delaware River. The park is in Pipersville (just north of Point Pleasant and about nine miles north of New Hope). You can use Google Maps to get directions to "High Rocks State Park, PA" although the directions below may still be useful for finding the parking lot.

- From the north (Riegelsville) via Rt 611 S: From Rt 611 S, turn left onto Rt 411 S. Continue about 1/4M to Pipersville, then turn left onto Dark Hollow Rd. Follow this over the Tohickon Creek, then about 1M later, turn right onto State Park Road. Follow this for about 1/2 M, then turn left onto Tory Road (a gravel road). A few hundred feet down this, turn left into the parking lot.

- <u>From the east (New Jersey) via Rt 202:</u> Follow Rt 202W across the Delaware River via a toll bridge. Make an immediate right turn and a left turn onto River Rd (Rt 32) North. From 32 N, follow the next set of directions. An alternative approach from Rt 202W is to take the Stockton Exit (sign indicates it is the last exit in NJ), take Rt 29 N into Stockton, turn left at the Stockton Inn, cross the bridge, and turn R onto 32N (at Dilly's Restaurant). Warning: The stretch of Rt 202 approaching the Delaware River is a notorious speed trap.

- <u>From the south (New Hope) via River Rd (Rt 32):</u> Follow River Rd (Rt 32) north to Point Pleasant. As you are entering Pt Pleasant, follow River Rd sharply right over a stone bridge (ignore the sign pointing left to Ralph Stover Park just before the bridge). Pass a general store on the left and make the next left onto Cafferty Rd. Continue for 1.8M, heading uphill and then passing Tohickon Valley Pk and Deerwood Campground on the left. After Deer Campground, make the next left turn onto Tory Rd. After 1M, Tory road branches off to the left and becomes a gravel road. Follow the gravel road for a few hundred yards and park in the parking lot on the right.

- <u>From the west (Doylestown) via Rt 611 N:</u> From Doylestown, follow Rt 611 N for about three miles and turn right onto Silo Hill Road (south) which shortly ends at Point Pleasant Pike. Turn left and follow Point Pleasant Pike into Point Pleasant. Turn left over the stone bridge onto River Rd (Rt 32) N, and then make the next left onto Cafferty Rd. Continue for 1.8M, heading uphill and then passing Tohickon Valley Pk and Deer Campground on the left. After Deer Campground, make the next left turn onto Tory Rd. After 1M, Tory road branches off to the left, becoming a gravel road. Follow the gravel road for a short distance and park in the parking lot on the right.

To reach the cliffs from the parking lot, enter the woods across the gravel road from the parking lot gate. Pass a warning sign and then follow the established descent trail that starts at the right-hand end of a detached section of wire fence and zig-zags down a gully leading to the west end of the cliffs. Please stay on the trail since it was painstakingly constructed to control erosion in the surrounding gully. Please do not descend the gulley itself.

A steep narrow face 35 feet high (conspicuously visible from the descent trail) contains the first route, Orvie. The routes descriptions are listed from left to right.

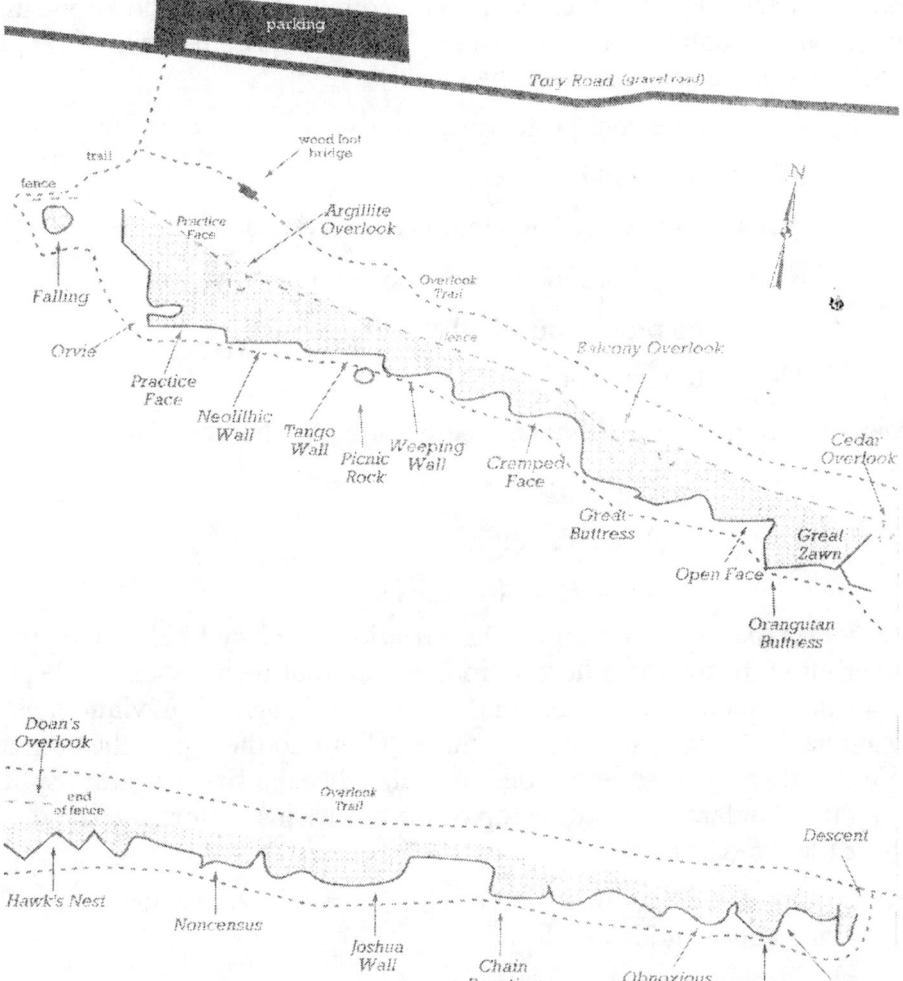

About The Route Descriptions

Routes have been graded using the U.S. system with a,b,c,d extensions for routes 5.10 and harder and +,- extensions for routes easier than 5.10. A split grade (i.e. 10d/11a) indicates that the difficulty is highly dependent on your height, the exact line you follow, or some other factor.

Leadable routes (other than sport climbs) have been given a protection rating as shown below. Protection ratings are merely an indication to assist you in deciding whether to even consider leading the route. It is still up to you to size up the route and decide for yourself whether you have the necessary skill and experience both at climbing and at placing protection to safely lead the route. This is especially true at High Rocks given the soft nature of the rock.

G	excellent protection
PG	reasonable protection
PG/R	somewhat bold, extra caution advised
R	very bold, poor protection and/or loose rock
X	no protection, skull and crossbones
TR	top-rope only

Many routes have been given a quality rating as shown below.

*	worth doing
**	well worth doing
***	genuine High Rocks classic

For routes that have variations, the variations are listed below the main description. In the main description, the point at which variations split from the standard route are marked with a "Var." abbreviation. For example, if the main description states "Climb to the top of the corner, (Var. 1) then traverse left.", this indicates that the first variation splits from the standard route at the top of the corner just before the standard route traverses left.

First ascent information is given below many of the routes using the following abbreviations.

FA	First ascent
FFA	First free lead ascent (without aid)

FLA   First lead ascent (top-roped previously)

FKA   First known lead ascent

FTR   First known top-rope ascent

After 1990, most first ascents are given the FKA assignment to suggest a lack of certainty.

About The Boulder Problem Descriptions

Boulder problems have been graded using the Hueco Tanks V-rating system which starts at V0 and increases in an open-ended fashion (V0, V1, V2, etc.) Boulder problems, by definition, are difficult and every fall is a ground-fall. Some problems have been given an R rating to warn of the potential for a particularly injurious landing or long fall, sometimes in combination with loose or friable rock or tenuous or difficult moves high off the ground. R-rated problems should be top-roped or otherwise attempted only by accomplished climbers who can complete the problem with no chance of a fall, although a group of competent spotters and crash pads can sometimes lessen the danger. Regardless of what the guide suggests, it is your sole responsibility to study the problem and determine the conditions under which you can attempt the problem safely, if at all. If you have any doubts, either do not attempt the problem or else use a top rope.

Recommended Climbs:

Traditional leading: *Airy Route* (5.3 PG/R), *Ivy Leaf* (5.4 PG), *Dead Tree* (5.5 G), *Hawk's Nest* (5.6 PG), *Tango* (5.8 PG), *Neanderthal* (5.8+ PG), *Obnoxious Partner* (5.8+ G), *Riff Raff Eliminate* (5.10a PG).

Sport climbing: Dean's List (9/11a), Tales from the Crypt (10a), Nameless Arête (10c), Noncensus Direct (10d), The Problem (12a).

Top-roping: all routes on the Practice Face (5.2-5.9), *The End Climb (Orvie)* (5.8+), *Neanderthal* (5.8+), *Obnoxious Partner* (5.8+), *Far Face Direct* (5.8+), *Phone Booth* (5.10a), *Stopper Ceiling* (5.10d), *Called On Account Of Pain* (5.11d).

Bouldering: Falling (V0+ R), Up (V1), Ripper Traverse (V2), The Low Traverse (V5), Marty Broke It (V8).

The Descent Trail

The first three climbs are visible from the descent trail.

1. **Falling** (V0+R) * A roof problem on the detached outcrop at the top of the descent trail, just below the fence. Pull the roof, but without using the blocks on the left. This is often top-roped because of the intimidation factor and unpleasant landing. A spotter is recommended even when using a rope because of the potential swing into the left-hand blocks.

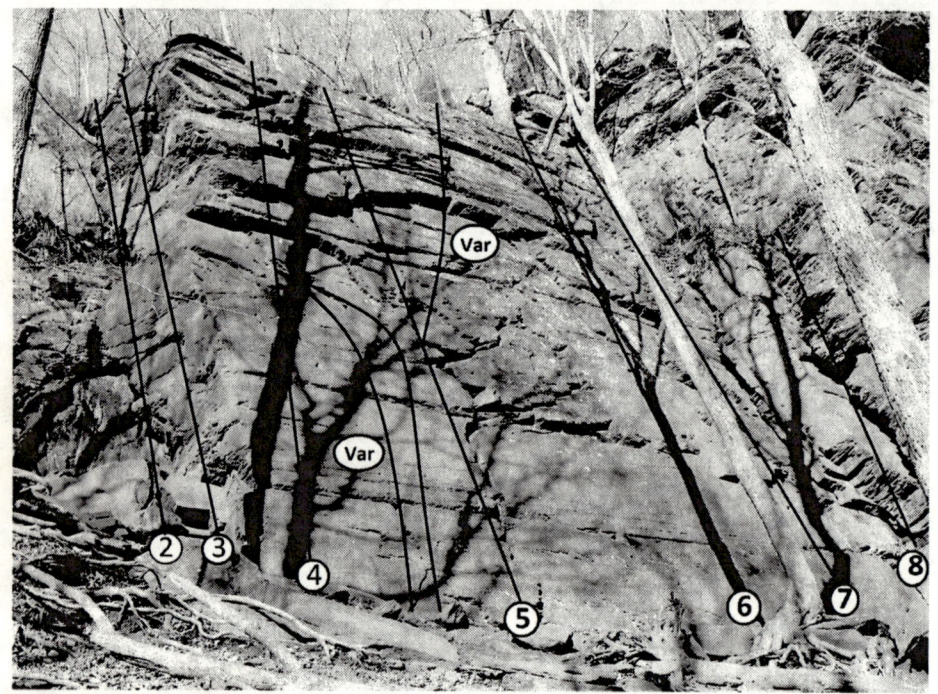

"The Practice Face"

2. **Orvie Direct** (9+/10a TR) * Begin below the steep, narrow face marked with "Orvie" graffiti at the far left end of the cliffs. The Practice Face is around the corner to the right. Straddle the sharp arête at the left edge all the way to the top. Difficulty depends on whether you use a big layback right of the arête and 8 feet above the half-way ledge.

3. **The End Climb (Orvie)** (8+ TR) ** Begin a few feet right of *Orvie Direct*. Climb thin edges up the center of the face to the half-way ledge (Var. 1), but without using the tempting corner on the right. (Var.2) Step left, then climb up and somewhat right reaching the top at a notch.
   Var. 1: (7) Use the arête on the right.

Var. 2: (9) From the half-way ledge, continue up slightly right of center.

The Practice Face

The most crowded area, typically festooned with top ropes because all the routes are moderate with fairly convenient anchors. To access the top, do not use the dank gully immediately behind the Practice Face because it is slippery and eroded. Instead, go a bit further back by a tree and scramble up a ledge system that is followed right and up to the top. Warning: do not use any single tree as an anchor since the roots are not as sound as they appear (see Hazards).

4. **Triple Overhang** (7 PG/R) * Start near the left edge of the Practice Face below three short parallel seams that slant up and left. (Var. 1,2) Climb up past the leftmost seam, then straight up through overhangs to the top.
Var. 1: (8 TR) Climb the center and right seams.
Var. 2: (9 TR) Climb the thin face between the right-most seam and the crack of Ivy Leaf.
FLA: Mike Cohen, mid-1960s.

5. **Ivy Leaf** (4 PG) * Climb the obvious crack in the center of the Practice Face until it ends. (Var. 1) Then move up and left through a notch to a small shelf, then up to the top.
Var. 1: (4) Move up and right to a vertical crack and climb this to the top.
FA: Joe Walsh, 1930s.

6. **Finger In The Dike** (6 PG) * Start at a smooth face between Ivy Leaf and the Practice Climb. Climb the right side of the smooth face past a short crack and a left-facing corner. Continue straight to top.

7. **Practice Climb** (2 G) * The crack near the right end of the Practice Face.
FA: Joe Walsh, 1930s.

8. **Practice Chimney** (5 PG) The dank chimney at the right edge of the Practice Face.

9. **Crank N' Up** (V0+) The right-hand corner of the Practice Chimney forms an overhanging arête with a plate-like jug reachable from the ground. Start hanging from the jug and

climb the arête 5 feet to a stance. Escape left. For your feet, everything is off-route except the overhanging portion of arête. Contrived but fun.

10. **Warmup Traverse** (V0+) * A long left-to-right traverse. Start at the Practice Chimney. Drop down and right below an overhanging bulge and continue traversing right, just above the ground, all the way to the start of the grungy Weeping Wall. Do laps if you wish.

11. **Shit Face** (10b TR) The narrow face just right of the Practice Chimney. Many variations can be done using the same top rope set up (accessible from the top of the Practice Face). (Var. 1) Starting just right of the Practice Chimney, climb an overhang to a small ledge. Then climb the center of a thin face to a small overhang (Var. 2,3), reach over this for holds, step right, and climb the right side of a short face to the top without using the outside corner on the right.
Var. 1: For a harder start, do the Mickey's Mantle boulder problem, then continue over the next overhang to the ledge.
Var. 2: (9) At the small overhang, step left and climb the left side of the face to the top (avoid the outside corner on the left).
Var. 3: (11a) At the small overhang, climb tiny edges up the center of the short face to the top.

12. **Mickey's Mantle** (V0) * Start under the lower overhanging bulge beneath Shit Face. From a near sit-down start, pull over the hang onto the awkward, sloping ledge.

The Neolithic Wall

The lower 35 feet of this wall is capped by a ceiling that provides the crux for the classic Stopper Ceiling and Neanderthal routes. Above the ceiling is the Neolithic Ledge which can be accessed by traversing right from the top of the Practice Face. The Neolithic Ledge is used both as a belay ledge and as a place to anchor top-ropes.

Climb High Rocks State Park 17

"The Neolithic Wall (Left)"

13. **Route 1** (4 PG) Begin at the left edge of the Neolithic Wall. Pitch 1: 55 feet. Climb the right side of the outside corner to a bolted belay on the Neolithic ledge. Pitch 2: 40 feet. Move up and left to a pie-slice shaped overhang, pass this on the right to a cedar tree and the top.
FA: Lou Lutz and Bob Chambers, Sep 1957.

14. **Route 2** (5/6 PG) Begin at a crack (crux) 8 feet right of Route 1 or at an easier crack 8 feet further to the right. Pitch 1: 65 feet. Up the crack to a small overhang with an old piton, then up through notch in the ceiling to the Neolithic ledge. Pitch 2: 35 feet. (Var. 1) Climb a left-facing inside corner to a higher ledge, then a corner and crack to an overhang. Step right, clear the overhang at some cracks shaped like the letter H. The second pitch is dirty and rarely done.
Var. 1: (7+) Climb to top via a spooky bulging ceiling split by a crack (directly above notch at end of 1st pitch).
FA: Lou Lutz and Bob Chambers; April 1958. FA (Var. 1): Mel Hamel and Tom Stryker, Nov 1978.

15. **Stopper Ceiling** (10d TR) ** A strenuous and challenging roof problem. Climb the thin face between Route 2 and Neanderthal to a small overhang, clear this at two loose flakes (9), then move up to the crux ceiling (at a dubious-looking bolt). Work out to the lip, hand traverse slightly right, then pull over and up to the Neolithic ledge. Although a top-rope is sometimes dropped from the top of the cliff, it is better to set an anchor from a bomber crack on the Neolithic ledge (medium to large cams and long slings needed).
FA: Unknown party using aid (A3), 1970 or 71. FTR: Unknown.

"Jeff Gagliano on Stopper Ceiling"

"Neolithic Wall (Right) and Tango Wall"

16. **Neanderthal** (8+ PG) *** A strenuous Stover classic, popular both as a top rope and as a lead climb. Pitch 1: 60 feet. Climb a crack up and into a conspicuous open-bottomed chimney, then swing out left to a stance below the crux notch in the ceiling. Grunt through the notch, then move up to a bolted belay at a cedar tree. Pitch 2: 45 feet. Climb the left-facing corner above the belay to the top.
FA: Lou Lutz and Bob Chambers, 1957. FFA: M.G. Block and Bob Dickson, 1957, possibly the hardest free climb in the Eastern US at the time. The archaic first-ascent bolts are still there below the crux ceiling.

"Climber on Neanderthal"

17. **Bootwear** (V4) Start to the right of Neanderthal and just left of a large left-facing inside corner. Edge up the blank face between two cracks until you can grab a small ledge about 13 feet up. The cracks are off route as are any holds that extend directly from the cracks (very contrived). This leaves only a few micro-edges for holds. New bootwear is helpful, as is a crash pad.
FA: Tom Stryker, 1980's.

18. **Bootbuster Ceilings** (8 PG/R) Starting just right of Neanderthal, climb the left-facing inside corner up to the ceiling just right of the crux notch on Neanderthal. Climb the ceiling (crux), then move up and left to a bolted belay at a cedar tree. Bring medium sized cams and thin crack protection.
FA: Bill Stevens and partner, 1963/64. FFA: Ed Stosky and Tom Stryker, 1977.

19. **Bootbuster Nose** V0 To the right of Neanderthal, from a sit-down start, climb a short, steep arête/nose to a ledge. Move left to descend. Potentially bad landing. Many variations possible.

20. **Picnic Rock Slab** (V0/V1) Climb a slabby groove to the top of the Picnic Rock boulder. Harder if you leave out the holds at the right edge of the groove. Potentially bad landing.

21. **Picnic Rock Toss** (V4) Sit down in the dirt below a small overhang on the side of the Picnic Boulder which faces the cliff (just left of the slab). Grab an undercling and a low flake, paste your feet on the rock and toss for the lip. A bad toss could fracture your spine unless you have a spotter.

The Tango Wall

Features the classic Tango (8) and some harder routes that go out the Tango ceiling.

22. **Hummingbird** (6 PG) * Pitch 1: (6) 70 feet, 1 bolt. Starting just right of a nose, climb a crack 18 feet to a small ledge. Climb a thin face past a bolt (crux), then work up past poor-quality rock until you can move right to a belay on a big ledge (the Tango belay ledge). Pitch 2: (4) 55 feet. Follow staircase-like shelves up left, place a large cam or hexagonal, then climb through an overhanging notch to the top (airy and exciting for the grade).
FA: Lou Lutz and Mike Cohen, 1963.

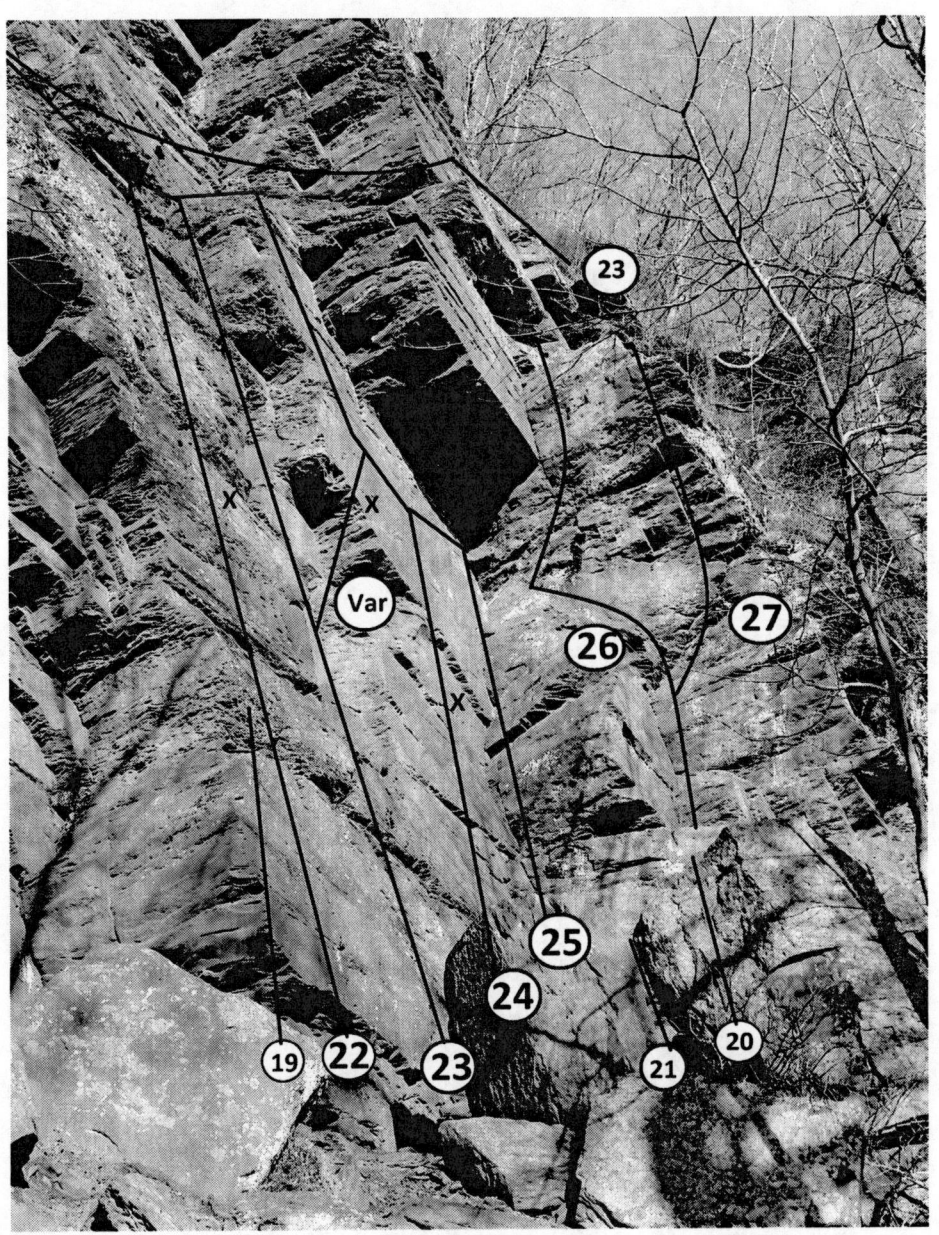

"The Tango Wall"

23. **Airy Route** (3 PG/R) * Pitch 1: 70 feet. Climb a crack for 20 feet, then awkwardly gain entrance to the cave crack (crux). Exit the cave, then step up right to the Tango belay ledge. Pitch 2: 40 feet. From the belay, traverse right

around the corner and up to another ledge. Scramble off right to a tree belay or climb straight up a face to the top.
FA: Joe Walsh, mid-1930s.

Note: A huge section of the Tango roof fell down during the first freeze of 2005 (the resulting block is embedded in the ground below and left of the ceiling). At one time, this was the site of the first 5.13 at High Rocks (Violent Femmes, FA: Colin Lantz, 1988?, original bolt above the lip) as well as the first 5.11 (Mass x Energy=Swing 11d, FA: Colin Lantz, Dean Hernandez and Jim Hall, 1985). These routes are completely gone. However, Gorilla is now much harder (see below)

24. **Tango Super Direct** (10a PG) * Start at a thin crack 8 feet left of Tango's left-facing inside corner. (Var. 1) Climb straight up 20 feet to a bolt, then make a long reach past a small overhang to gain a shelf below the large Tango ceiling. Finish on Tango.
Var. 1 (9-): Start by Airy Route and then move up right past a bolt (left of the bolt on Super Direct) to reach the left edge of the shelf below the Tango ceiling. Finish on Tango. This variation is now popular because the bolted anchors at the top are directly above it.
FA: Tom Moffat and Mel Hamel, July, 1982.

25. **Tango** (8 PG) ** A High Rocks classic. Pitch 1: (7) 70 feet. Climb a large left-facing corner to a shelf below the Tango ceiling. Equalize some fixed pitons, then traverse left along the shelf until it is possible to pull up into a left-facing inside corner (crux, harder if short). Continue up and step right to a belay ledge. Pitch 2: (8) 35 feet, 1 bolt. From the belay, climb straight up a steep left-facing inside corner to a ceiling that is passed on the right.
FA: Mike Cohen and Stu Bartram, 1964.

26. **Gorilla** (11d PG) Start 8 feet right of the Tango corner. Climb a short right-facing inside corner (or the overhangs just left of it) moving left to a ledge at the right edge of the big roof. Pass the big roof on the right via the finger locks in the corner.
FA (original 5.7 route):Lou Lutz and Bob Chambers; May 1957

"Climbers on Tango"

27. **Crummy Rotten Crack (CRC)** (10b R) Follow Gorilla up the initial corner to a larger corner. Move out right to the bottom of a thin overhanging crack just left of the outside corner. Staying left of the outside corner, climb the crack past an old piton to the top.
FA: Mike Werner, Spring 1975. FFA: Bill Shaniman, 1978 or 79.

28. **CRC Groove** (V0 R) Start around the big corner right of Crummy Rotten Crack. Just right of the arête, from a sit-down start at two low-holds, climb the groove just right of the arête without using the arête. Traverse off to the left.
Var. 1: Advanced Warmup Traverse (V1) Climb CRC Groove then reverse the "Warmup Traverse", along the way, completing *Bootbuster Nose*, *Mickey's Mantle* and finishing up on *Crank N' Up*.

The Weeping Wall

A wet and grungy section of rock to the right of the Tango Wall. Because the rock is so poor, there are no routes except for an ugly route with a bolt that is probably not worth doing (and is not described). The next clean section of rock is the New Generation buttress.

"The Weeping Wall"

29. **New Generation** (8 PG) * This route has a tree directly in front of it. Pitch 1: 40 feet, 1 bolt. Climb a dihedral that

starts 5 feet above ground, then swing out right to a stance. Move left to the bolt, then fire straight up the steep, thin, exciting face passing the final overhang on the right (or pull over it via a notch, harder). Belay on the ledge (bolts). Pitch 2: Follow a fourth class gully on the left to the top.
FA: John Geiger and Tom Stryker, Oct 1978.

The Cramped Face

The next section of cliff is a big, less-than-vertical, 100' tall face capped by overhangs. The first two climbs start just left of the face on a ledge 12 feet above the ground.

30. **Loose Block** (3 PG) 80 feet. Start just left of the Cramped Face on a ledge 12 feet above the ground. Climb the left-facing inside corner and crack (crux) to a stance (Var. 1, 2). Angle up and left following the easiest ledges and corners to the top.
Var. 1 Loose Block Direct (5+ PG) Continue in the main corner until you can step right to a large belay ledge. Climb the corner above the left side of the belay (crux) to a ledge with a cedar tree. Behind the tree, climb a short face past a piton to the top.
Var. 2 Blockhead (6+ PG) * Continue in the main corner until you can step right to a large belay ledge. Directly above the belay, climb a steep awkward dihedral to a ledge with a cedar tree. Behind the tree, climb a short face past a piton to the top.
FA: Joe Walsh, 1930s. FA (Var. 1): Joe Walsh, 1940s.

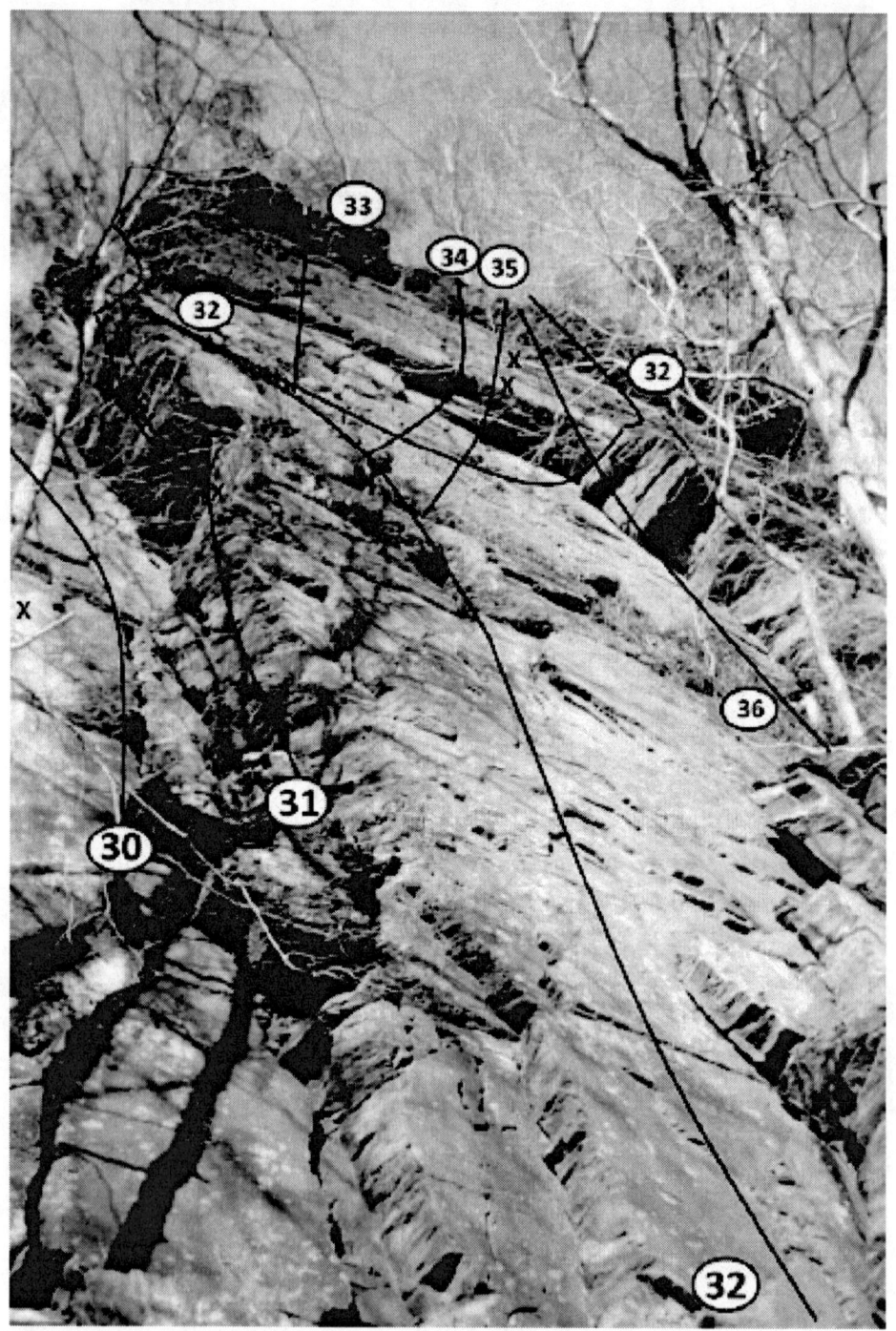

"The Cramped Face"

31. **Shalestorm (10b PG)** * Start as with Loose Block. Pitch 1: (10b) 40 feet, 4 bolts. (Var. 1) Climb the steep, narrow, friable face just right of the Loose Block corner and gain a ledge beneath a ceiling (8R). Alternatively, climb Loose Block up to this point (easier and safer). From beneath the right side of the ceiling, reach out to the lip, pull the ceiling, then follow bolts up the center of an overhanging face to a large belay ledge (#2 Camelot). After clearing the ceiling, if you reach right to the arête to rest, that reduces the grade. Pitch 2: (6+ PG) 40 feet. (Var. 2) Same as Blockhead variation of Loose Block.
FLA: Paul Nick and Greg Roper, Dec 1993.
Var. 1: To the left of the Loose Block corner is a blank slab with a bolt near the top. **Var. 2: (8 PG)** From the belay, step right around the corner and climb the Director Overhang.

32. **Cramped Thumb** (6 R) An adventurous route. While the crux moves have reasonable protection, there are exciting run-outs, dubious pitons and poor rock. Start at a small left-facing inside corner at the base of the Cramped Face. Pitch 1: (6) 60 feet. Climb the thin face just left of the small corner past a bent pin, then move up and right to a notch in an overhang. Clear this, then follow a groove up to a narrow ledge with old pitons. This was the original belay; however, it is safer to traverse left around the outside corner to a more secure belay (#2 Camelot). Pitch 2: (5) 70 feet. Traverse far right, passing below a ceiling until you can swing around an awkward corner to a ledge. Follow a dirty crack up and left to the top. It is possible - perhaps even recommended - to do the route in one pitch.
FFA: Francis DeMonterey and John Gyer, 1963.

33. **Director Overhang** (8- PG) * Follow Cramped Thumb to the narrow ledge with old pitons. Climb straight up to the overhang that caps the left side of the Cramped Face and clear this at an obvious notch.
FA: Bob Chambers and Lou Lutz, late 1950's, approached crux overhang from belay ledge on Loose Block.

34. **Cramped Thumb Direct** (8 PG/R) * A nice route, but a bit bold to lead. Follow Cramped Thumb past the notch in the

overhang. Angle up and slightly right to the crux notch in the overhang. There is an astonishing collection of pitons here. Equalize them! Clear the notch and finish on a steep exposed face with old pins.
FA: Mike Cohen, 1963 or 64.

35. **After Burner** (10d PG) Start as with Cramped Thumb Direct, but diverge right and under the ceiling with a bolt above the lip. Clip the bolt, turn on your after-burner, pull the lip and head past another bolt to the top.
FA: Bob Markland, Mike Flood, around 2000.

36. **Higher Than I** (7 PG/R) A grungy, worthless epic. The first pitch is often overgrown with vines. Begin below prominent vertical cracks just above the trail. One crack is wide enough to accept your entire body. Pitch 1: 60 feet. Climb the cracks to a vegetated ledge. Walk left 25 feet to a stout belay tree at the right edge of the Cramped Face. Pitch 2: 70 feet. Straight above the tree, climb a large left-facing inside corner to a ceiling. Clear the ceiling (old piton above it) and go straight up the dirty face to the top.
FA: Dave Ainsley and John Meyers, Fall 1977.

The Great Buttress

The tallest section of the cliffs. Almost all the routes here include a belay on the Cactus Ledge, a long ledge equipped with several two bolt belays. The Cactus Ledge can be accessed via a series of class four ramps to the left of the Open Book route, but traversing this ledge unroped is dangerous because a slip would be fatal.

37. **Three Buttresses** (5 PG/R) * A nice route with an exposed second pitch. The sheer mankiness of the pitons near the top adds additional spice. Start below a shallow open book that starts 8 feet above the trail. Pitch 1: (4 G) 60 feet. (Var. 1) Climb the open book most of the way (Var. 2) and step right onto a ledge. Move up to a tree belay. Rappel or... Pitch 2: (5 PG/R) 55 feet. Climb a corner/crack to a small ledge, then move up a steep and crumbly face past an old piton to an overhang. Move out right (exposed!) and up to the top.

Var. 1 **Nonsense**: (7 R) Begin 10 feet right of the regular start. Climb the unprotected face moving up and left past a small corner with small bush jutting from it, then up steeper rock to a ledge. Step left to the tree belay.
Var. 2: (5) Continue up the open book to overhangs, then hand traverse right to the tree belay.
FA: Joe Walsh and party, late 1940's.
FA (Var. 1): Warren Musselman and Holly Abbott, March 1983.

"The Great Buttress (Left)"

"Jeff Gagliano on Wild Wall with Tohickon Gorge in Background"

"The Great Buttress (Center)"

38. **Open Book** (2 G) Just left of Tales From The Crypt, climb an open-book to the Cactus Ledge.
FA: Joe Walsh, Winter 1941 (solo).

39. **Cyfleusterau** (7 R) Don't bother with the rusted-through piton at the crux - just girth hitch a clump of the plentiful poison ivy vines. Start at the left end of the Cactus Ledge. Climb a large right-facing corner for 10 feet, then move up and right into a steep left-facing inside corner (with the rusted through piton). Make airy, exciting crux moves up and right to gain ledge. Climb a chimney clogged with a dead tree to the top.
FA: Tom Stryker and Tom Schilder, Nov 1982.

40. **Wild Wall** (9 R) The crux is the groove that splits the very center of the overhanging bulges that cap the Great Wall. The direct line is loose and scary. Start at the 2 bolt belay on the left side of the Cactus ledge above Tales from the Crypt. Climb the short left-facing corner and move left and up past a series of pancake flakes to a loose ledge with a bolt. Climb the crux groove directly above the bolt to the top.
FA: Tom Moffat and Dean Hernandez, around 1989.

41. **Tales From The Crypt** (10a) ** With retro-bolting, the route is now well-protected and has some great face climbing. You can find it behind a tree above a narrow section of the trail. Pitch 1: 60 feet, 3 bolts. Follow the bolts to a large ledge with a bolted belay (the Cactus Ledge) (Var.1). Rappel or... Pitch 2: (7 R) 60 feet, 2 bolts. Step across the Cactus Ledge to the right-most 2-bolt anchor, then climb up through a notch protected by a bolt (Var. 2). Follow your leading instincts up past another bolt to an exposed slab (5 R) that is followed to the top (Var. 3).
Var .1 (11/12a): Several variations are possible on the thin holds left of the second bolt.
Var. 2: Wild Wall Finish (9 PG/R) * The complete linkup is the best multi-pitch outing in the area, although perhaps not for the faint of heart. The second pitch is for experienced and solid traditional leaders only. After moving through the notch above the Cactus Ledge,

diagonal up left until at the bolt below the crux notch on the Wild Wall. Finish on Wild Wall.

Var. 3: Sinestra (7 R/X) Instead of climbing the exposed slab, keep left and climb the left side of the exposed arete that forms the right edge of the Wild Wall. This variation provides a great photo opportunity from the overlook.

FA: Mel Hamel and Tom Stryker, Sep 1979, route sieged using only a knife-blade and a poor nut placement to protect the crux. At one point, Hamel perched himself on a block weighing several hundred pounds just below the crux in order to rest. The block cut loose, thankfully missing the belayer, and Hamel was left dangling eye-to-eye with a bat who was not pleased at the loss of its hang-out.

FKA (Var. 3): Michael Flood, 1995.

42. **Dean's List** (9/11a) ** 60 feet, 4 bolts. Start up the large inside corner just right of Tales From The Crypt until you can step right to clip the first bolt (Var. 1). Thereafter, if you use the arête as common sense dictates, it is 5.9. If you completely avoid the arête, it's about 5.11a.

Var .1 (Crumble For You): (10d) At the top of the initial corner on Dean's List, move up into a smaller inside corner with an old fixed piton. Clear the roof at the top of corner and continue up. This was an established route here before Dean's List, but with Dean's List nicely bolted a few feet to the right, it is hard to imagine anyone wanting to do this except as a top-rope variation.

FA: Dean Hernandez, 1993.

FA (Crumble For You): Marty Trumbore and Tom Moffat, Oct 1984.

43. **Friable Alternative** (8 R) * 60 feet. Superb pitch, but fairly bold! Bring steady nerves and a versatile rack. Start below a low overhang between Dean's List and the cave-like crack on Rattlesnake. Surmount the overhang, then angle up and slightly left past a small overhang to a smooth and solid face. Move up and right through the final overhangs at a notch, then step left to the Cactus Ledge bolted belay. PS: If I find any bolts on this, I will personally remove them!

FA: Tom Moffat and Tom Stryker, Mar 1981.

"The Great Buttress (Right)"

44. **Rattlesnake** (7 PG/R) * Starts below a cave-like crack. Pitch 1: 70 feet. Climb into the cave-like opening, then exit onto the face above. Continue up, climb through a notch in an overhang and gain an alcove with a museum grade pin. Traverse left to Cactus Ledge 2-bolt belay. Rappel or... Pitch 2: 35 feet. Traverse back right and awkwardly gain a slot that splits the overhangs above. Exit the slot up and right, then find the most secure path to a belay at a cedar tree up and left of the slot. Pitch 3: 50 feet. Follow an easy vegetated gully system to the top. Some do not bother with last two pitches that tend to be grungy, but the moves at the start of the 2nd pitch are airy, awkward and exciting making them perhaps the crux of entire route.

FA: George Austin and Roland Machold, Spring 1954.

45. **Riff Raff Eliminate** (10a PG/R) ** 80 feet. Although protection can be found (small wires important), this is only recommended for leaders solid at the grade. Begin below a left-facing inside corner at the right end of the broad face containing Rattlesnake. Climb the corner to a ceiling (Var. 1). Step left, then edge and stem up a steep corner (crux) to a cramped alcove below overhangs. Traverse far left beneath the overhangs to the Cactus Ledge bolted belay and rappel. Rock fall recently increased the difficulty of this route.
Var 1. (Zig Zag) (8 R) Included for historical purposes and has no other redeeming qualities. Pitch 1: Follow Riff Raff up the initial corner to the ceiling (crux). Whereas Riff Raff now steps left, instead step right around the outside corner. At a rusted through piton, climb the grungy face (4 X) moving up and left to belay on a ledge above the top of the Riff Raff crux corner or anywhere you can find a reasonable belay.
FA: Tom Moffat and Chris Lesher, May 1980. The initial ascent stepped right and up instead of traversing far left to the Cactus Ledge, however, the original route is not recommended.
FA (Var. 1, Zig Zag): Lou Lutz and Bob Chambers, Feb 1957.

Open Face and Orangutan Buttress

This section is identifiable by a tall, wide open, fairly low-angle face split by a prominent gully (the Open Face route). This is a popular spot for rappelling. The Long Chimney route separates the right edge of this face from the Orangutan Buttress.

"Open Face"

46. **Open Face** (5 R) 110 feet. The prominent gully going up the center of the huge face. Protection is sparse.
FA: Joe Walsh, late 1930s

"Orangutan Buttress"

47. **Open Face Slab** (7- PG/R) 110 feet. Climb the face 6-8 feet right of Open Face past three bolts to the top. The first bolt is high up and protection below it is mediocre. A safer alternative is to climb Open Face and step right on a ledge that is slightly below the first bolt. This was led sans bolts by an unknown party in the 1980's.

48. **The Long Chimney** (3 PG) * 95 feet. The first technical rock climb established at High Rocks. Climb the chimney at the right edge of the Open Face to the top.

FA: Joe Walsh, mid-1930s.

49. **Dandy Line** (8 PG/R) This exciting and adventurous climb gets steep and exposed near the top. The top-out itself will make your hair fall out. Beware of poison ivy. Pitch 1: Follow Long Chimney about 2/3 of the way until you can step right onto a belay ledge. Pitch 2: 45 feet. To the right of the Long Chimney, climb a parallel vertical crack system to the top.
FA: Chris Lesher, Tom Moffat and Mike Moffat, Apr 1984.

50. **Orangutan Traverse** (V3) ** Interesting and unusual moves makes this much better than it looks. Start at the very bottom of the Long Chimney and traverse right about 25 feet, just barely off the ground. After reaching a big right-facing flake, move awkwardly up and right into a dihedral and exit right.

51. **Orangutan** (8 R) * A historical classic, over-vegetated in summer. Beware of poison ivy. Starts 25 feet right of Long Chimney at an 8 feet high corner. The crux is the prominent "Crack of Doom" at the top of the buttress. Pitch 1: (3 R) Climb easily up the nose past a piton. At the second ledge, (Var .1) move right and up to large belay ledge (fixed piton above ledge). Pitch 2: (8) (Var. 2) To the right of the piton, climb an overhanging bulge to a stance and then up the "Crack of Doom" to the top.
Var. 1: Continue up the nose to the belay ledge.
Var. 2: (5.9 TR) About 6 feet left of the standard finish, climb the bulge and overhanging face, then up a thin crack to the top.
FA: George Austin and Roland Machold, 1954.

Climb High Rocks State Park 41

"Upper Great Zawn Gully"

52. **Super Slab** (11a TR) This improbable route surmounts the jutting ceiling that caps the right side of the Orangutan buttress. Begin on a broken up ledge system that can be accessed by climbing partially up the Great Zawn gully

(described below) and traversing left. Climb a clean corner to an overhang that is passed on the right. Continue up a face to another overhang split by a crack (fixed piton). Clear the overhang to gain an alcove below the big jutting ceiling. Pull up to the lip of the ceiling, then pull onto the slab (crux). This was led for the first ascent; however, there was a bolt on the final slab that is now missing.
FA: Mark Ronca, 1992.

53. **The Great Zawn** (Class 4) To the right of the Orangutan buttress is a Class 4 gully known as the Great Zawn. The very top of the gully can be dangerous, especially if the rock is wet or one is weighted down by a pack filled with gear. The next two climbs are located on an overhanging wall near the top of this gully.

54. **Man Of Science** (12c/d) 30 feet, 5 bolts, anchor. The left-most sport climb on the overhanging wall at the top of the Great Zawn gulley.
FLA: Michael Flood, Summer 1996.

55. **The Problem** (12a) ** 30 feet, 4 bolts, anchor. The right-most sport climb on the overhanging wall at the top of the Great Zawn gulley. A bit run-out near the top. FLA: Dean Hernandez, 1993.

Garden of Eden Buttress

Contains a number of obscure climbs that are rarely done. Some of the climbs start 40 feet above the trail on a large ledge system called the Garden of Eden Ledge. This ledge system can be reached by climbing the first pitch of Adam (3) or by climbing part-way up the Great Zawn and then traversing cautiously to the right along a ledge system.

56. **Grungy Green Thumb** (V0 R) 20 feet. Climb the short lichen-covered wall to the left of a left-facing inside corner to a vegetated ledge with a tree. This and the next route have been totally reclaimed by green grunge.

57. **Grungy Green Thing** (5 PG) Start at a left-facing inside corner at the right edge of short lichen-covered wall. Climb the corner and exit up left to a vegetated ledge with a tree.
FA: Matt McMillan and Tom Moffat, Summer 1981.

"Garden of Eden Buttress (Left)"

58. **Adam** (3 PG/R) The first pitch is okay, but the second is revolting. Start 20 feet right of Grungy Green Thing in a large left-facing inside corner with several trees. Pitch 1: (3 G) 40 feet. (Var. 1) Climb the corner up through a notch to the Garden of Eden Ledge. Pitch 2: (3 PG/R) 55 feet. Scramble left and up to higher ledge below the left edge of the buttress. Follow a dirty, broken up groove/crack up right, then step left to a stance beneath a notched overhang. Climb the overhang and the left-facing inside corner above to the top.
Var. 1: (6 PG/R) Climb the unprotected but pleasant face left of the initial corner.
FA: George Austin and Roland Machold, 1954.

59. **Eve** (6 PG/R) Pitch 1: Same as Adam. Pitch 2: 35 feet. (Var.1). Climb the major dihedral that splits the buttress to the top.
FA: George Austin and Roland Machold, 1954.
Var. 1 (5.5 PG) Climb the crack immediately right of the dihedral rejoining the standard route at the top.

60. **The Outsider** (5.8) Start on the big ledge halfway up the cliff. From a tree belay, climb the slabs up left to the first bolt at an overhang. Follow the left-hand line of bolts to the top.
FLA: Bob Markland, 1999

61. **Raising Cain** (5.11a/b) If you are short, expect a very scary clip at the crux. Start on the big ledge halfway up the cliff. From a tree belay, climb the slabs up left to the first bolt at an overhang (Var. 1). After the first bolt, move up right to a double bolt, and continue to follow the right-hand line of bolts past the crux overhang to the top. Resting on Adam reduces the difficulty.
Var. 1 (5.12a): At the roof, don't reach out left, instead move desperately out right.
FLA: Paul Nick, 1997

62. **The Serpent** (9+ R) 35 feet. Start from the tree belay on the Garden of Eden Ledge. Look for an intimidating overhanging groove near the top of the buttress to the left of Eve. Scramble up left and climb a thin crack out a small ceiling, directly below the overhanging groove. Continue up and climb the groove itself.
FA: Chris Lesher and Tom Stryker, Nov 1980.

63. **Leshtovers** (7+ R) 35 feet. Obscure, spooky and wild for its grade. (Var.1) Follow Serpent over the initial ceiling, but instead of climbing the overhanging groove, veer right and follow a diverging groove out right and up to the top.
FA: Mel Hamel and Tom Moffat, Summer 1981.

64. **Outcast** (9-) 3 bolts. 35 feet. Follow three bolts over two overhangs between Leshtovers and the main dihedral of Eve.

65. **The Wizard Of Maz** (10d R) 40 feet. Start from the tree belay on the Garden of Eden Ledge. To the right of Eve, climb the right-hand overhanging fist-crack to a marginal stance (strenuous). Continue up and right to the top. With big cams, the protection is decent through the crux, but there is still a loose, strenuous and scary run-out at the end.
FA: Mel Hamel and Tom Moffat, Summer 1981.

The next two routes start from a ledge with a large bush below a face capped by overhangs, about 40 feet right of the Garden of Eden Ledge. It can be accessed by traversing right from the Garden of Eden ledge (roping up recommended) or by scrambling up the Class 4 gully to the left of Welcome To Stover and then moving carefully left.

"Garden of Eden Buttress (Right)"

66. **My Brother's Leeper** (7 R) 35 feet. The crux originally sported a Leeper-Z piton. The rock is of the poorest quality imaginable. From the ledge, climb friable rock out left and up to a 10 foot groove, then climb this past a rusty piton to a bulge. Continue up to an overhang formed by rotting flakes and surmount this at a loose crack. FKA: Tom Ellix and Tom Moffat, 1979.

67. **ADB Overhang** (8 PG/R) 35 feet. From the ledge, climb a well protected left-facing inside corner to the ceiling. (Var. 1) Step left and surmount the ceiling via an exciting loose notch.
Var. 1: (9 PG/R) Pull directly over the big ceiling that caps the corner. Wild and strenuous.
FA: Tom Moffat and Mel Hamel, Sep 1981.

FKA (Var. 1): Paul Nick, 1992.

Hawk's Nest Area

To the right of the Garden of Eden area is a band of overhanging rock with many chalk-coated flakes. At the left end is a class four gulley often used as a descent route for roped climbs in the area. This area contains the best and most challenging bouldering at High Rocks including the popular Ripper Traverse. The landing area contains rocks jutting out of the ground, so uncontrolled bouldering falls are dangerous, particularly without a spotter.

68. **Dave 66** (V3 R) Caution advised. Starts at a small cave left of the descent gulley. From the left side of the cave entrance, climb straight up the thin face above the cave entrance.
Var 1: (V0- R) An easy warm-up circuit, but don't fall from it. From the left side of the cave entrance, climb big jugs up and left, then descend on the left via a ramp, then traverse back right near the bottom to the starting point.

69. **Ripper Traverse** (V2) ** For full credit, start by straddling the gully at the left end and then traverse right about 35 feet to easy ground below the Hawk's Nest route. The holds are mostly big, but the terrain is steep and pumpy. V2+ is for the path of least resistance, but many variations increase the difficulty.

70. **Up** (V1/V2) * Just to the right of the gully at the left end is an overhanging bulge. Start about 5 feet right of the gulley. Work up to a pair of thin incut edges and deadpoint for the sloping top, or reach for it statically if you are tall and strong. Use a spotter and check out the landing area before attempting.
FA: Tom Stryker.

71. **Up And Up** (10d R) 30 feet. Do the Up boulder problem (crux), then surmount the big jutting overhang above (fixed piton in fragile rock).
FA: Mark and Carla Ronca, 1992, piton pre-placed by reaching down from above.

72. **Battle of the Bulge** (V2 R/X) Very bold, spotters recommended. Starts between Up and Welcome To Stover. Climb up past the right side of an overhanging nose.

"Hawk's Nest Area (Welcome to Stover)"

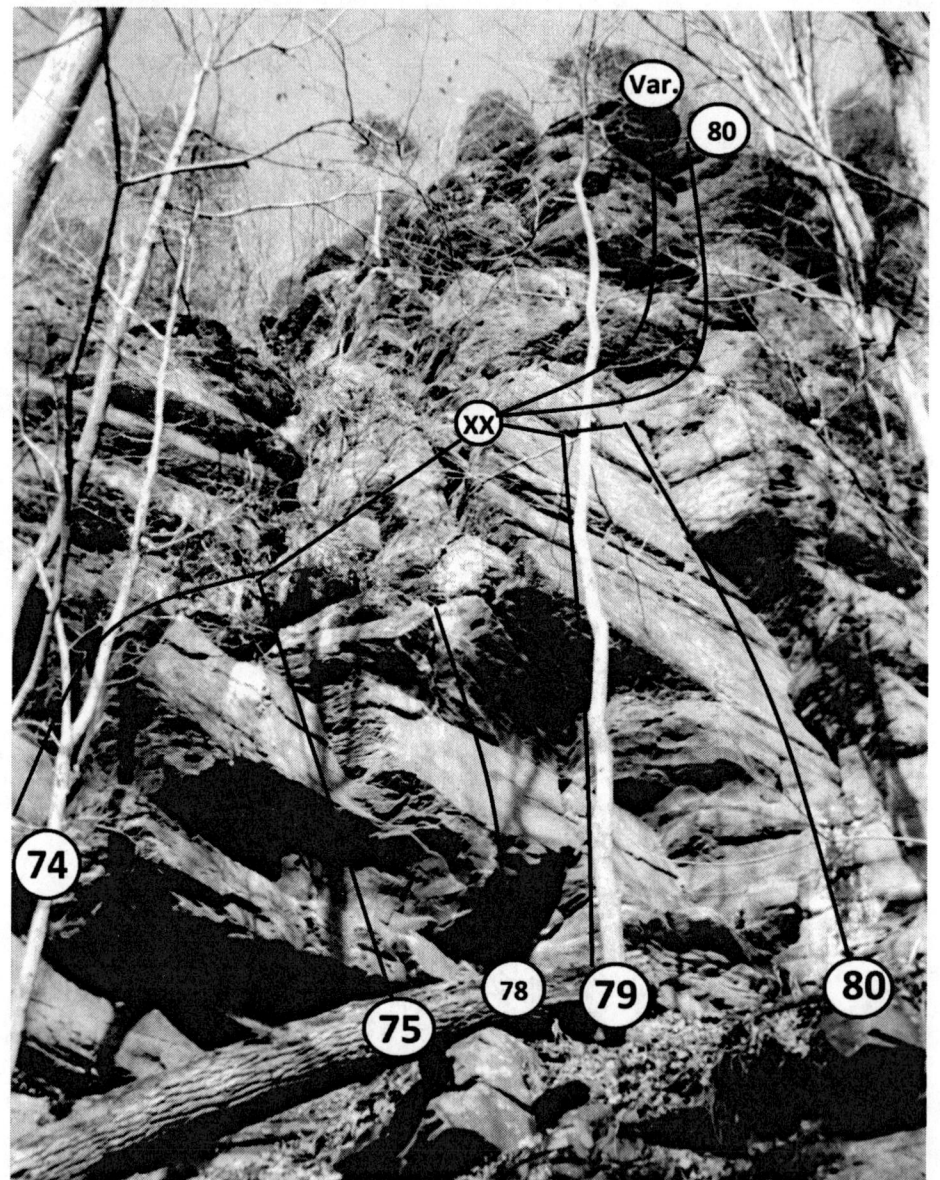

"Hawk's Nest Area (Hawk's Nest)"

73. **Welcome To Stover** (10d) ** 25 feet, 2 bolts. Short, but hard. Follow the bolts up to and over the ceiling.
FA: Tom Stryker, May 1981.

74. **Foot Free And Fancy Loose** (7+ PG) * 40 feet. Pull up into the left-facing inside corner just right of Welcome To Stover. Traverse right via the under-cling, then move up to a ledge. Walk right to a clean corner and climb this to a 2 bolt belay on Hawk's Nest. To get down, scramble off left to the class four descent gully.
FA: Paul Tiers and Randy Wolf, Oct 1978.

75. **Multiple Arrests, No Convictions** (10b/c R) 35 feet. Start 8 feet right of Foot Free below a small alcove 9 feet above ground with a fixed piton tucked in the back. Gain the alcove from the right and pull the overhang above onto a short face (Lowe tricams useful here). Pass left around a bulge to a ledge. Follow Foot Free to the 2 bolt belay.
FA: Tom Stryker, Mel Hamel and Tom Moffat, Mar 1982.

76. **Ripper Up** (V3) * Reverse the Ripper Traverse and finish on Up.

77. **The Low Traverse** (V5) ** The best of the Ripper Traverse variations. Goes right to left as close to the ground as possible. Two difficult sections, each a problem by itself, are separated by a rest spot. For the right half, squat down under the celing at the far right end where the Ripper Traverse finishes. Starting from a jug, move left using holds on and below the underbelly of the lowest ceiling (but not those at the ceiling's lip) until you have gained the rest position at the start of Welcome To Stover. For the left half, continue left using a blocky undercling and the small, fingery holds just above the lip of the lowest overhang. Requires strong fingers and precise footwork.
Var.1: The right half can also be traversed using the pancake flakes at the lip.
FA: Mike Donahue, 1995.

78. **Stand and Deliver** (V5 R) Just left of Hawk's Neck, climb an overhanging nose to a very thin face.
FA: Colin Lanz, 1980's.

"Paul Nick on Low Traverse", Photographer: Vicky Schwartz

79. **Hawk's Neck** (8 PG/R) * 50 feet. The protection is better than it appears from the ground. Start 10 feet left of Hawk's Nest at a short crack capped by a ceiling. Climb the crack and pull directly over the ceiling at a thin seam (8) or skirt around the ceiling on the left or right (easier). Continue up the center of the face past a blank section (8, crux), then step left to a 2 bolt belay. Scramble off left to the descent gulley or try Variation 1 of Hawk's Nest.
FA: Tom Moffat and Bob Lyon, 1979.

80. **Hawk's Nest** (6 PG) ** The first pitch is classic. The second is a bit grungy but okay for adventure. Start below a conspicuous open book that begins 10 feet above the trail. Pitch 1: (6) 50 feet. Climb up into the open-book (crux), then move up to a ceiling. Step left and climb a corner with a crack to another ceiling. Traverse left to a 2 bolt belay. Pitch 2: (4) 50 feet. (Var. 1) Traverse right around the ceiling and follow a chimney to the top.
Var. 1: (7 PG/R) From the 2-bolt belay, move up and slightly right over a small overhang with a rusty piton. Climb another overhang at a notch, then either rejoin the regular route or continue straight to the top.
FA: George Austin and Roland Machold, 1954.

81. **Ronca's Roof** (8 R) 75 feet. Although the crux roof can be protected, this route is a horror show due to loose and friable rock. Climb the chimney just right of Hawk's Nest to a ledge with a tree. Continue up right and climb an overhang at a seam and notch.
FA: Mark Ronca and Michael Flood, May 1992.

82. **Slap** (V2) * An exciting problem, spotter recommended. To the right of Hawk's Nest is an overhanging arete that forms the right edge of a chimney. Slap your way up the arete, but after reaching the obvious big jug up high, bail off into the chimney. For full credit, start low and don't get help from across the chimney.
FA: Chris Lescher, 1980's.

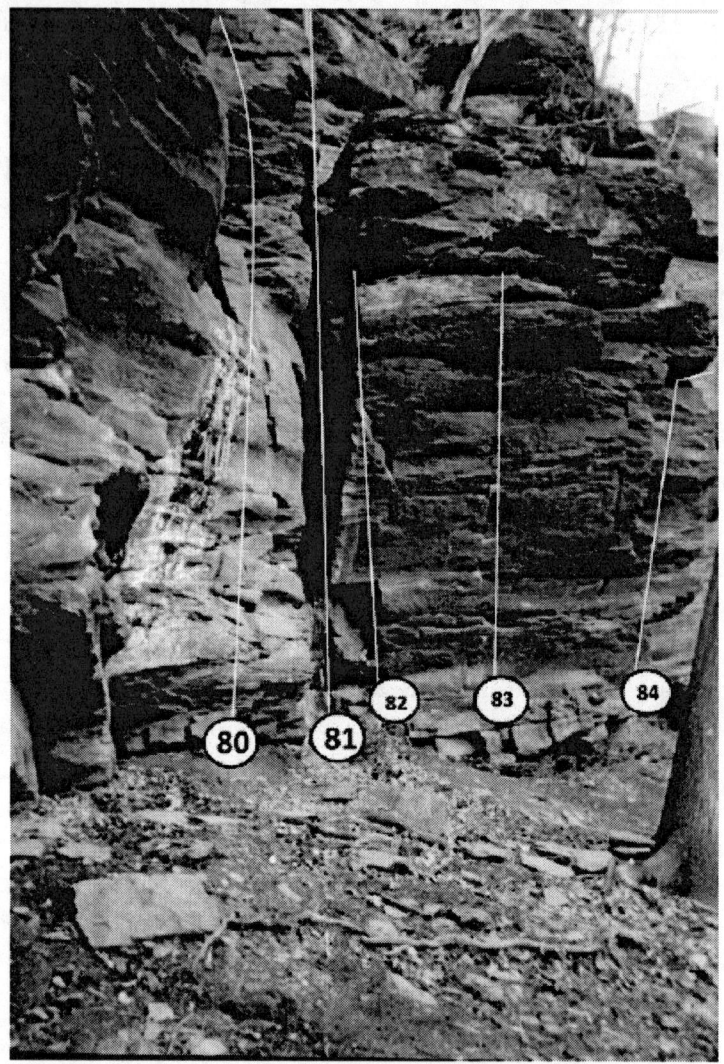

"Hawk's Nest Area (Marty Broke It)"

83. **Marty Broke It** (V8) * This testpiece was once easier, but then Marty Trumbore broke off a key hold. Climb the center of the bleak, overhanging face to the right of Hawk's Nest. Height dependent.
FA (post-Marty): Colin Lanz, late 1980's.

84. **Haul** (V2) Begin on bigger holds just right of Marty Broke It. Climb overhanging rock to a marginal stance just below

the loose looking flakes at the top. At this point, forget the dangerous loose flakes and bail off to the right.
Var. 1: A variation is possible going up the seam just to the left.

85. **Hidden Hang** (V0-/V1) This bouldering outcrop is well-hidden below the trail. To reach it from Hawk's Nest, head down towards the stream angling left until it is possible to cut back right. Hidden Hang features an overhang, 15 feet wide and 8 feet above the ground. Numerous variations can be done including traverses. Bouldering to the top of the outcrop is not recommended because the upper face is extremely dirty.

86. **Crack Magic** (5 G) 35 feet. Starting 25 feet right of Hawk's Nest, climb the crack in the left-facing corner.
FA: John Geiger, Tom Stryker and Les Burnett, 1977.

87. **Cramped Cosmonaut** (10a TR) Climb the thin crumbly face a few feet right of Crack Magic.

88. **Technicolor** (8 PG/R) 35 feet. Start at a short nose 10 feet right of Crack Magic and just left of a short inside corner capped by a ceiling. Climb the nose and continue up left past a fist-sized crack and a shallow left-facing corner to a ledge.
FA: Chris Lesher and Harry Waters, 1979.

"Hawk's Nest Area (Crack Magic)"

89. **Speechwriter Blues** (7 PG) 35 feet. Flakes resembling shark fins jut from the trail below this route. Start below a short, smooth, left-facing inside corner capped by a ceiling. Climb the corner and move left past the ceiling to the top.
FA: Matt McMillan and Steve Hunt, around 1982.

90. **New Jersey Turnpike** (V4 R) 20 feet. Rarely done because it's scary and bold. Boulder the vertical groove just right of Speechwriter Blues using many spotters.
FA: Mel Hamel, 1980's.

Noncensus Area

The Noncensus route is located where the undercliff trail becomes little more than a narrow ledge with a steep drop-off below.

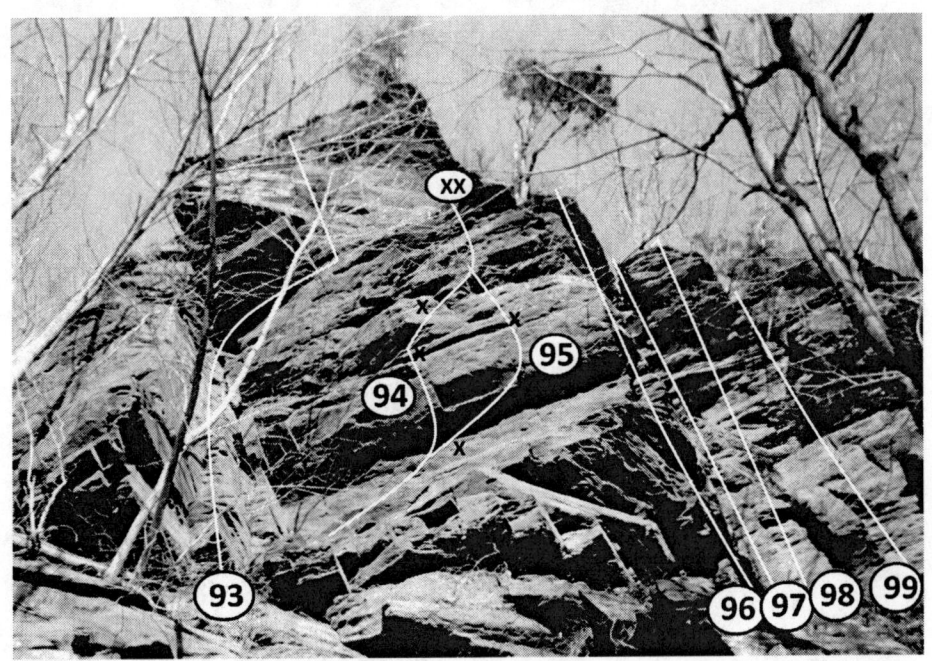

"Noncensus Buttress"

91. **The Diamond** (10c TR) * Climbs a roughly diamond-shaped buttress above a vegetated ledge that is 40 feet above the trail and just left of the Noncensus buttress. Rappel the top rope to reach the vegetated ledge. The best belay is at a tree even with and 20 feet left of the route's base. Start up the left side of the buttress, and as the rock leans back to a very steep angle, angle up and right until you can climb straight to the top. Harder variations on the buttress are possible.

"The Diamond"

92. **Hollywood & Vine** (5.8 R/X) Climb up just left of the nose, which is right of the Noncensus corner. Continue up a broken crack to the top. Other variations with dubious protection have also been done around here.
FKA: Mike Flood, 1994?

93. **Noncensus** (9 R) 90 feet. Where the undercliff trail narrows to become a ledge, climb a left-facing inside corner until just below and left of a triangular overhang. Traverse right below the triangular overhang, then move up right to a stance. Climb a thin face up and left past a ledge to the top or move right to the chains on Noncensus Direct.
FA: Tom Moffat, Tom Stryker and Mel Hamel, Aug 1983.

94. **Noncensus Direct** (10d) 35 feet. Climb the left-hand line of bolts on overhanging rock, moving right near the top to the chains. Getting to the first bolt is run out.
FLA: Bob Markland, 2002?

95. **Noncensus Redirect** (12) 35 feet. Climb the right-hand line of bolts to the chains. The first bolt is shared with Noncensus Direct.
FLA: Bob Allen 2002?

96. **Nothing Yet** (8 R) 80 feet. Start just left of a major corner (Oh Promise Me) below a fixed piton that is 12 feet above the ground. Angle up and left on steep rock and big holds to a small dihedral near the nose. Climb the dihedral (crux) to a stance, then follow the easiest path up and left to the top. The fixed piton is difficult to clip and its failure could have harsh consequences.
Var. 1: (8 TR) Climb directly over the piton and continue up the face to the top.
FA: Tom Stryker and Tom Moffat, Mar 1981.

97. **Oh Promise Me** (4 PG) * 65 feet. Climb a large left-facing inside corner up through a chimney to the top.
FKA: Warren Musselman and friends, Feb 1979.

98. **Intimidation Syndrome** (10a PG/R) 60 feet, 2 bolts. Contrived. Starting just right of Oh Promise Me, climb a crack to a ledge beneath a narrow bulging overhang. Climb the overhang past two well-spaced bolts to the top.
FA: Mark Ronca, Dec 1993.

99. **The Hearth** (5.8 PG/R) 60 feet. Start 12 feet right of Oh Promise Me below a short, smooth, slightly overhanging face that begins 10 feet above the ground and is lined on both sides by vertical cracks. Climb past the overhanging face to a ledge, then move up and climb a small overhang at a fist-sized crack. Step up and right onto a ledge, then up a right-facing inside corner to the top.
FA: Tom Moffat and Tom Ellix, Thanksgiving 1978.

100. **Don Juan** (11b) 20 feet, 1 bolt. A short, overhanging nose with a bolt on the right side. Stick-clip the bolt.
FA: Marty Trumbore and Dean Hernandez, circa 1989.

101. **Geiger Sanction** (6 PG) 55 feet. A good route marred by some loose rock near the top. Climb a large right-facing corner immediately right of the overhanging nose of Don Juan. 30 feet up, make an awkward move right to gain a ledge below a ceiling. Move out right and up to the top.
FA: John Geiger and Tom Stryker, May 1978.

102. **Falling Cedar** (7 PG/R) 55 feet. Over-vegetated due to lack of traffic. 12 feet right of Geiger Sanction, climb a small right-facing corner, then follow a seam over a small overhang. Continue up and slightly left to the top.
FKA: Mark and Carla Ronca, Dec 1994.

103. **Jammin** (1 G) 35 feet. Just left of Squatting Room Only, climb a crack on the left side of a chimney to the top.
FKA: John Anderson, 1981 (solo).

104. **Squatting Room Only** (6+ R) * 60 feet. This is a worthwhile lead, but only if you are rock solid in the grade. Above where the trail becomes very narrow, follow a cramped corner system that leans awkwardly to the left. Bring small wires (that tend to pop out as fast as you put them in) and a cam for the slot in the ceiling.
FA: Dave Ainsley and John Meyers, July 1977.

Joshua Wall

A steep wall with a bolted route, a ceiling 30 feet above the ground and a cave-like crack starting at ground-level at the right end.

Climb High Rocks State Park 59

"Joshua Wall"

105. **New Testament** (11a) *** 60 feet, 3 bolts. A fantastic route that starts with a tricky boulder problem and finishes with a wild ceiling. Unfortunately, at the time of writing, the fixed protection above the upper ceiling was not within reasonable clipping reach. Starting below the first bolt, climb up flakes, then make tricky moves past the thin face (crux). Move up to the ceiling (small tcu's helpful) and fire it to the top. FA: Dean Hernandez, 1990.

106. **Joshua 1:9** (7 R) * 65 feet. At the right end of the Joshua Wall, climb a cave-like crack to a stance above it. Traverse delicately left on a narrow shelf past a bolt. Climb up under the left side of the ceiling, surmount the ceiling at a thin crack and continue to the top.
FA: Dave Ainsley and John Meyers, July 1977. Bolt added after the FA, and it's still scary!

107. **Epitaph** (6 PG/R) 50 feet. Loose and well-named. Starting just right of the Joshua Wall, scramble up low-angle ramps to a crack in a short left-facing inside corner capped by an overhang. Climb the corner, pass the overhang on the right, and continue straight to the top.
FA: Matt McMillan and Warren Musselman, Oct 1981.

Chain Reaction Buttress

A steep buttress separated from the Joshua Wall on the left by a section of grungy, 4th class rock. The left end of the buttress has a overhanging bolted arête.

108. **Wham, Jam, Thank You Cam** (6 G/PG) 40 feet. Start on a convenient ledge with a tree, 15 feet above the trail and just left of a bolted arête. From the ledge, climb the left-facing inside corner past a crack, a ledge and an overhang to a stance near the top. Traverse left until you can sling a tree and pull over the top.
FKA: Doug Reilley and Robert Romanowicz, May 1992.

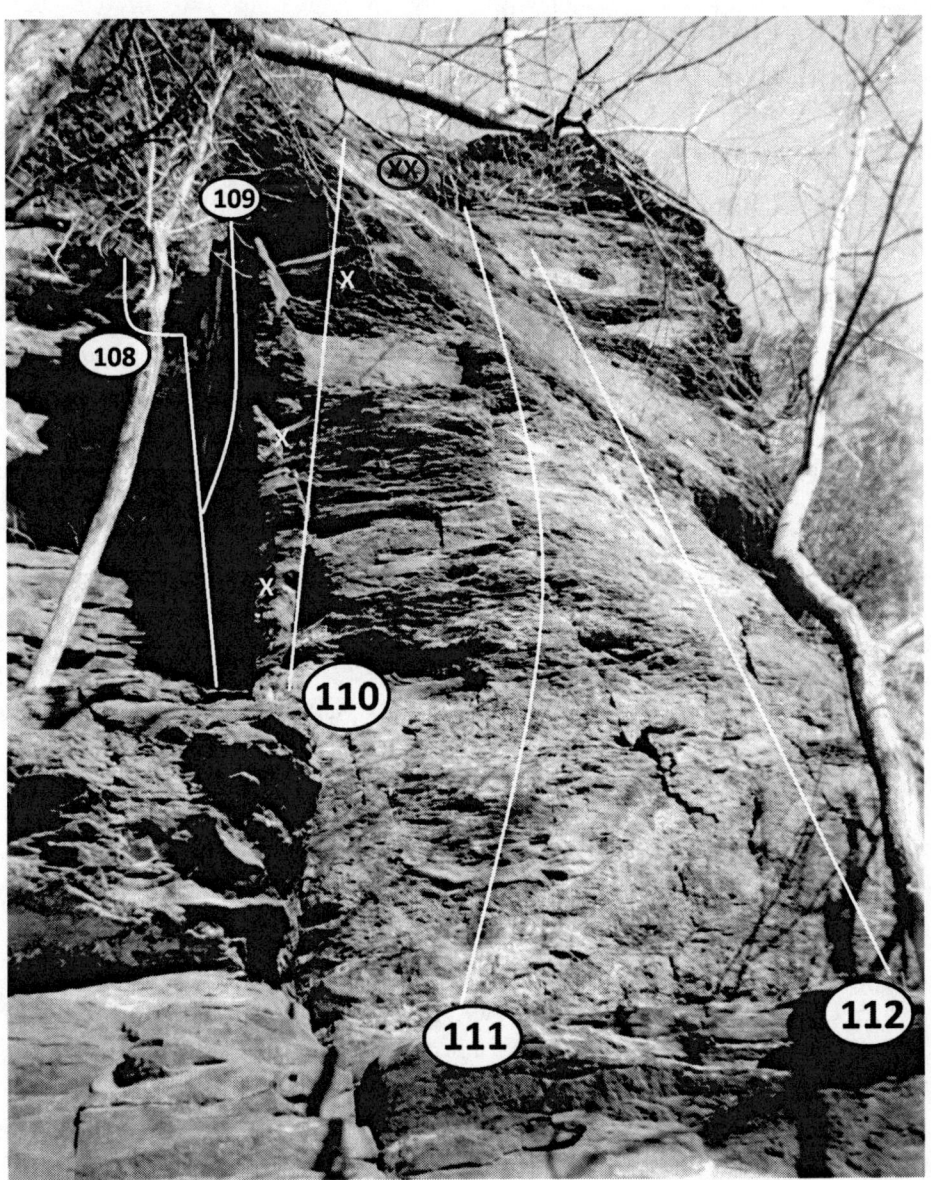

"Chain Reaction Buttress (Left)"

109. **Just A Stem Away** (8 PG/R) Not a bad route when dry. Follow Wham, Jam up the initial crack and corner to a stance, then charge up the exciting, overhanging face on the right without stemming across the corner. Pull into a small alcove up and right, then move up and left to the top.

FKA: Doug Reilley and Robert Romanowicz, May 1992.

110. **Nameless Arête** (10c) ** 35 feet, 3 bolts, shuts. A bolted arête that starts from the same ledge as Wham, Jam.
FLA: Dean Hernandez, 1994.

111. **Chain Reaction Direct** (10d TR) 35 feet. A goodtop rope to do after leading the Nameless Arête. Start below the steep face just right of the bolted arête. Pull awkwardly onto a narrow shelf at a point 9 feet below a very small right-facing corner. Climb steep rock straight up past the corner to the anchors.

112. **Chain Reaction** (10a X) 35 feet. Start on a ledge 15 feet above the ground. Climb up fractures to a small stance, then angle up and slightly left to better holds. Continue to a ledge with anchors.
FA: Colin Lantz, Warren Musselman and Andrew Lust, Oct. 1984.

113. **Deaf and Dumb** (4 PG) 75 feet. Start at a large chimney/gully 12 feet past the Chain Reaction Buttress. Climb the left-facing corner until forced left by a ceiling. Climb up to another ceiling (Var. 1), then exit right and up to the top.
Var. 1: (6 PG/R) Move out left and up around the nose to a bulging overhang. Climb this angling up and right to top.
FA: Frank and Carl Abissi; Spring 1978.

114. **Beautiful Loser** (10a R) 75 feet, 1 pair of bolts. Often infested with poison ivy. If you fall from the steep slab at the top, the bolts won't prevent you from hitting the ledge. Starting 12 feet right of Deaf and Dumb, climb a short bulging face to a large ledge. Approach the pair of bolts above from the right, then clear the overhang onto a steep slab and continue to the top.
FA: Mel Hamel and Tom Moffat, Fall 1981, bolt placed on lead.

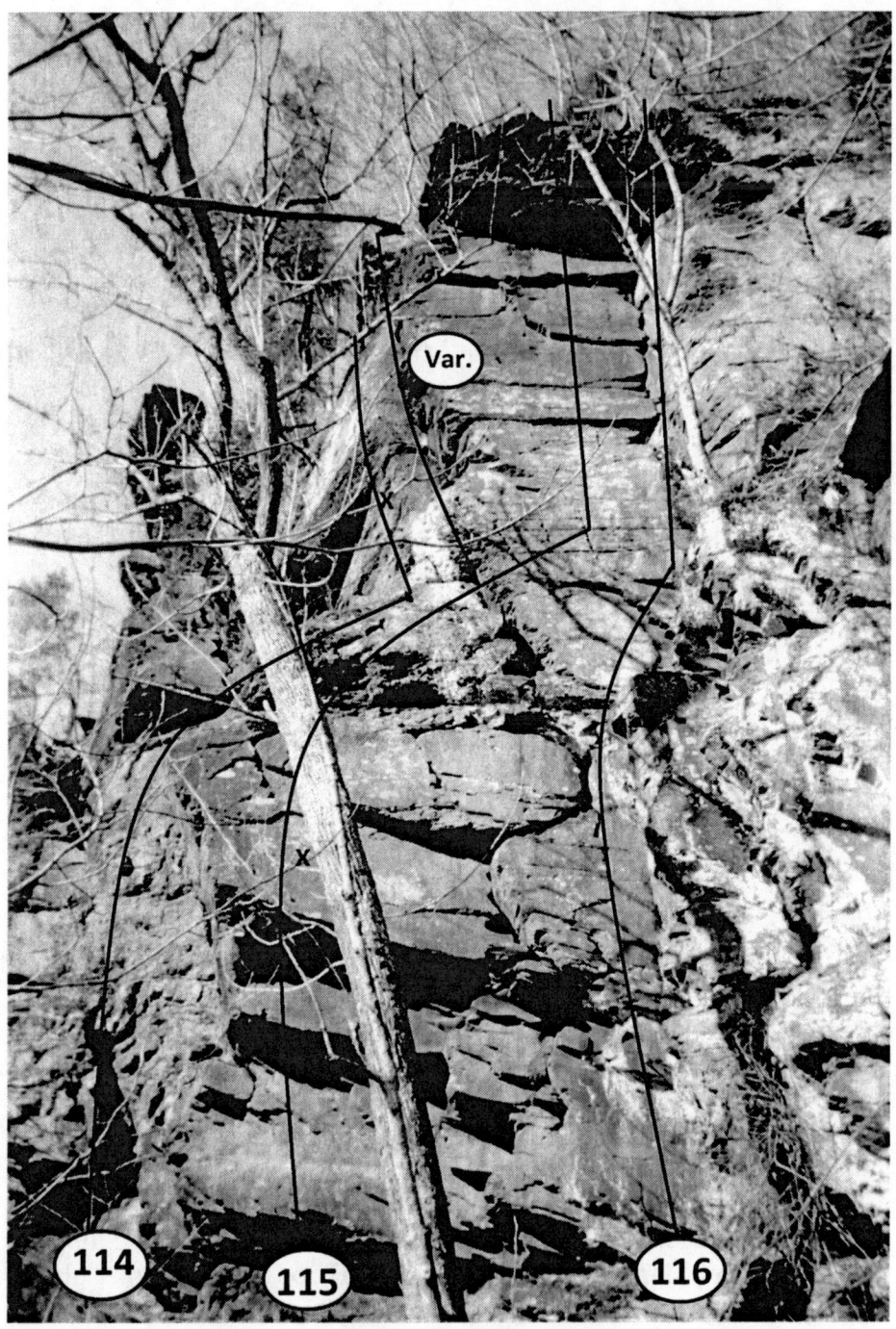

"Chain Reaction Buttress (Right)"

115. **Games Without Frontiers** (9+ PG) * 75 feet, 1 bolt. Start below a tiered overhang with a bolt just above the second overhang. Go up and clip the bolt, then crank past the short face above (crux) to gain a ledge (Var. 1). Place protection for the second, then traverse right and climb the center of a pleasant face past a fixed piton to some overhangs that are climbed via a notch in the center.
Var. 1: **La Dolce Vita** (7- PG) Instead of traversing right, climb a corner directly above to the top.
FA: Warren Musselman, Aug 1982 Original bolt placed on rappel.
FA (Var. 1): Warren Musselman and Rick Moffat, June 1981.

116. **No Self Control** (6 G) 70 feet. Just right of Games Without Frontiers, climb a large corner past a ledge with a tree, then up through a notch in the final overhang.
FA: Warren Musselman and John Anderson, Oct 1981.

117. **Zipperama** (8 R) 45 feet. Start 8 feet left of Old Chimney below a short, steep face. Climb the face 14 feet to a ledge, then follow a seam to the top. Bring small wires and Lowe-Balls or other small sliders.
FKA: Mark and Carla Ronca, Dec 1994.

Obnoxious Partner Buttress

Contains the classic overhanging fist-crack known as Obnoxious Partner. This buttress is separated from the Phone Booth Buttress on the right by a large chimney.

118. **Old Chimney** (1 G) 45 feet. An easy chimney 18 feet left of Obnoxious Partner.

119. **Run Out Of Favors** (9+ R) 45 feet. Poor quality rock and questionable fixed protection. To the left of Obnoxious Partner, climb a crumbly, bulging overhang past a piton to a ledge, then up steep rock past another piton to the top.
FA: Mark Ronca and Michael Flood, 1992, pitons placed on rappel.

"Obnoxious Partner Buttress"

120. **Dead Tree** (5 G) * 45 feet. 12 feet left of Obnoxious Partner, climb a right-facing inside corner to a big roof, then traverse left and up to a ledge. Climb a slightly overhanging fist-crack to the top.
FKA: Tom Chianese and Jim Henry, Oct 1977.

121. **Hook, Line And Swinger** (8 A3) 45 feet. The last remaining aid climb. Start below a large roof to the immediate left of Obnoxious Partner. Climb the face up to

the left-most seams in the roof. Aid the seams to the lip, then climb the face above to the top.
FA: Mark Ronca and Geoff Buhn, 1992.

122. **Obnoxious Partner** (5.8+ G) *** 45 feet. Climb the conspicuous overhanging fist crack. Tricky, strenuous and extremely popular.
FA: Unknown, the identity of the original obnoxious partner has been lost to history.

Phone Booth Buttress

Easily recognizable by wildly overhanging rock. On the right side of the buttress is a vertical face known as the Far Face.

123. **Short Face (V0-)** Left of the Phone Booth buttress is a short clean face leading to a thin crack in a small overhang.

124. **Called On Account Of Pain** (11d) ** Steep and strenuous! Begin below the left side of the overhanging buttress. (Var. 1) Move up and left towards the big chimney until it is possible to hand traverse out right onto overhanging rock. Climb to the top staying near the left edge of the buttress. Var. 1 (direct start): (12a) Start by pulling directly over the initial roof at a small notch.
FTR: Dean Hernandez, 1986.

"Phone Booth Buttress"

"July Engiles on Phone Booth", Photographer: *Vicky Shwartz*

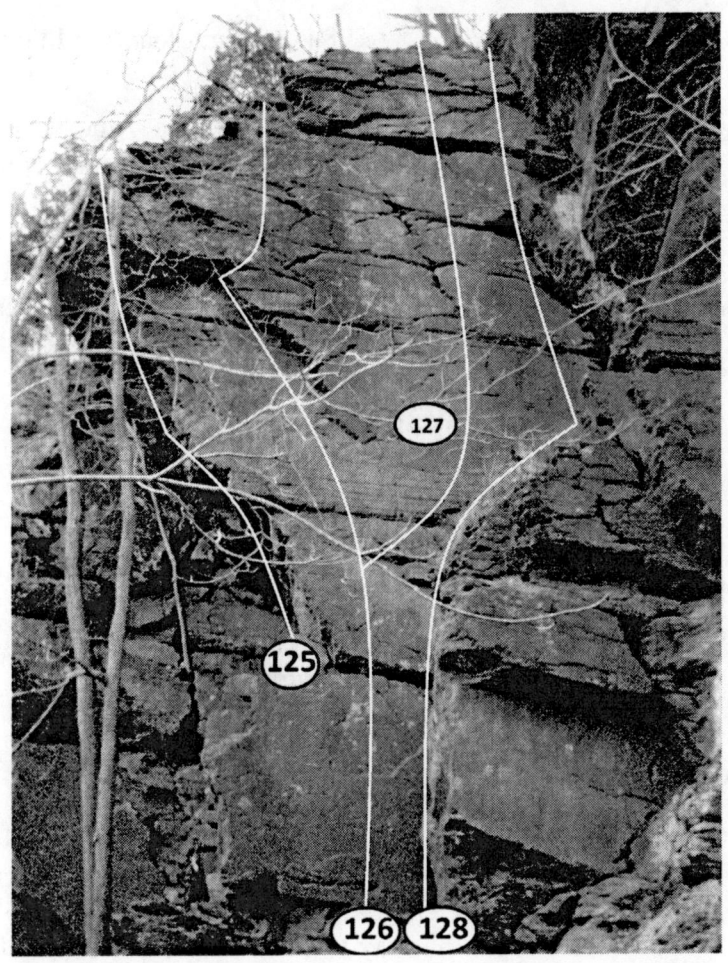

"Far Face"

125. **Phone Booth** (10a TR) *** Begin on a ledge below the right edge of the overhanging buttress. (Var. 1, 2) Climb the left side of the edge until you can angle left into the Phone Booth alcove (Var. 3), then continue up a corner on the right to the top.
Var. 1 (direct start): 5.10c Start 6 feet left of the edge and pull the ceiling direct.
Var. 2 (traverse): 5.10d Start as with Called On Account Of Pain and traverse up and right into the alcove.
Var. 3 (left finish): 5.10c From the alcove, move left and up to the top.

FLA: Paul Craven, Oct 1984, on sight lead while on tour of U.S. from U.K.

126. **Far Face** (7 PG/R) * 45 feet. Start below the vertical face on the right side of the Phone Booth Buttress. Climb the left-facing corner or the tricky face just left of it. Move up and left to a small left-facing inside corner near the left edge of the face. Move up the corner, then shift a bit right and up to the top. Although this is rarely lead, the protection is reasonable once you reach the small inside corner.

127. **Far Face Direct** (5.8+ TR) * 50 feet. Start same as Far Face but move up and right and climb weaknesses directly up the center of the face to the top.

128. **Far Face Corner** (4 PG) 55 feet. The main left-facing corner at the right edge of the Far Face.

129. **The Last Stand** (9+ TR) * This top-rope problem climbs the right end of the overhanging face to the right of Far Face. Strenuous and worthwhile despite loose holds. If you use the ledge above and left of the lower start, it's about 5.8. You can also go up where the bolt is, also about 5.8.

130. **The High Rocks Girdle Traverse** (10d) It is not clear that this 18-pitch epic has ever been repeated in its entirety. It starts by climbing Obnoxious Partner past the crux. Then it traverses left all the way to the Practice Face. 12 of the 18 pitches are 5.8 or harder. The complete route description can be found in the 1985 guide-book, *Red Rock: A Climber's Guide To High Rocks*; however, if you feel compelled to take this voyage, why not make up your own route?
FA: Tom Moffat and Mel Hamel, Fall 1981, completed as a series of separate pitches climbed over several days.

"The Last Stand"

Grey Rocks

This is a more remote area reached after a 15 minute hike from the parking lot. The cliffs have a gray color that is noticeably distinct from the main cliffs. From the parking lot, step into the woods and turn left onto the over-cliff trail. Follow this trail roughly parallel to the river, passing the top of the Phone Booth Area. When the trail splits, stay right. The most fool proof way to find Grey Rocks is to wait until the trail starts to cross a very obvious rocky stream bed. Turn right and follow the stream bed a short distance. When the water flows off the edge of the outcrop to form a mini-waterfall, turn right and descend via a short wide gully. The river is now directly in front of you. Many possibilities for moderate climbs exist on these cliffs. Only the more distinct or challenging lines are listed. Facing the cliffs at the water fall, the moderate climbs are on the left and the harder climbs are on the right.

"Grey Rocks (Left)"

131. (5.0-5.1) 25 feet. Climb the big easy corner or the slightly harder face left of it to the 2-bolt anchor.

132. (5.6 PG) 25 feet. Climb the face on the right side of the prow past a short crack to the 2-bolt anchor. If leading, bring tiny nuts.

"Grey Rocks (Center)"

133. (5.8- R) 35 feet. Harder and more interesting than it looks. Climb the face on the right side of the blunt arête through the low overhands and past some thin climbing to the top. If leading, bring tiny nuts, huge cams and steady nerves.

134. (5.11c) * 25 feet, 2 bolts. Climb the arête past the two bolts finishing on the left side. Small cams and/or small to medium nuts are helpful to protect the final moves.
FLA: Dean Hernandez, 1993?

135. (5.10b) Start just right of the arête directly below a knife blade piton with a cord on it. Climb straight up past the piton to the flakes and on to the top.
FLA: Dean Hernandez, 1986?.

74   Climb High Rocks State Park

"Grey Rocks (Right)"

136. (11a/b) 25 feet, 3 bolts. Height dependent. Start from the same position as the previous climb, but down low, step right and climb the thin face past three bolts to a small ceiling and then the top.
FLA: Dean Hernandez, 1994?

137. (5.9 PG/R) 25 feet. Climb up into the left-facing corner just right of the previous climb, then move past the shelf hold (crux) to the top.

Further right, there is a mysterious single bolt on a very blank lichen-coated face.

Red Rocks Remote

This area consists of a series of discontinuous outcrops, one of which has a prominent roof. To get to this area, you take the same trail as to Grey Rocks, but continue, crossing the rocky stream bed. The trail curves uphill to the left, and in a few hundred feet a smaller trail splits to the right. The most fool-proof way to get to the cliffs is to take the smaller right-hand trail to the right and continue until you see the cliffs (facing you) off to the left. The easier way that involves less scrambling is to stay on the main trail (red dot in white square), which heads uphill to the left. When the rise in the trail comes completely to an end, the cliffs are just to the right (facing away form you below).

138. (5.7 G) 25 feet. Starting near the left edge of the face, climb a discontinuous series of cracks that trend rightward.

139. (5.10a) 25 feet, 2 bolts. Take the line of most resistance and climb the thin face left of the bolts, passing a horizontal, and eliminating the easier cracks on each side. The bolts appeared around 2000, but this had been led ground up in 1995 by the author and probably earlier by others.

140. (V2) Several bouldering possibilities are encountered walking right from the previous route. The best one starts from a jug beneath a low overhang with thin holds above it. Surmount the overhang and descend the groove to its right.

76   Climb High Rocks State Park

"Red Rocks Remote (Left)"

"Red Rocks Remote (Right)"

141. (5.8 G) 30 feet. This climb and its variation are good if you enjoy ceilings with burly top-outs. Easy climbing leads to a ledge and then a crack through a small ceiling (Var. 1).
Var.1 (5.9+) 1 bolt. Climb the ceiling at the bolt, just left of the crack.

142. (5.11 TR) 20 feet. Right of the previous route, there is a tree growing against the cliff, with a narrow right-facing wall to its right. Starting at double-cracks, climb the awkward wall staying away from the left-hand arete.

143. (5.9- G) 30 feet. It's all arms on this one. Climb the major weakness at the left edge of the big ceiling (Var. 1). Approach directly from below.
Var.1 (5.6) Climb the chimney groove to the left.

144. (5.10d TR) 30 feet. Climb straight up through the big ceiling on its left side.

145. (5.10a/b PG) 35 feet. Climb out the ceiling via the prominent right-arching crack to the scary looking hanging-flakes on the right (Var. 1). The flakes are more solid than they appear; however, as always, climb at your own risk.
Var.1 (5.8- PG): Approach the hanging flakes from the right.

INDEX

Adam (3 PG/R) 43
ADB Overhang (8 PG/R) 45
After Burner (10d PG) 30
Battle of the Bulge (V2 R/X) 46
Beautiful Loser (10a R) 62
Called On Account Of Pain (11d) ** 66
Chain Reaction (10a X) 62
Chain Reaction Direct (10d TR)........................ 62
Crack Magic (5 G) 53
Cramped Cosmonaut (10a TR)........................ 53
Crank N' Up (V0+)............... 15
Dandy Line (8 PG/R) 40
Dave 66 (V3 R)..................... 46
Dead Tree (5 G) * 65
Deaf and Dumb (4 PG) 62
Don Juan (11b).................... 58
Epitaph (6 PG/R) 60
Eve (6 PG/R)........................ 43
Falling (V0+R) *................... 14
Falling Cedar (7 PG/R) 58
Far Face (7 PG/R) * 70

Far Face Corner (4 PG)........ 70
Far Face Direct (5.8+ TR) * 70
Finger In The Dike (6 PG) *............................ 15
Foot Free And Fancy Loose (7+ PG) *............... 49
Friable Alternative (8 R) * 35
Games Without Frontiers (9+ PG) * 64
Geiger Sanction (6 PG)........ 58
Grungy Green Thing (5 PG).............................. 42
Grungy Green Thumb (V0 R) 42
Hawk's Neck (8 PG/R) * 51
Hawk's Nest (6 PG) **......... 51
Hidden Hang (V0-/V1) 53
Hollywood & Vine (5.8 R/X) 57
Hook, Line And Swinger (8 A3)................. 65
Intimidation Syndrome (10a PG/R) 57
Ivy Leaf (4 PG) * 15
Jammin (1 G) 58

Joshua 1:9 (7 R) * 60
Just A Stem Away
  (8 PG/R) 61
Leshtovers (7+ R) 44
Man Of Science (12c/d) 42
Marty Broke It (V8) * 52
Mickey's Mantle
  (V0) * 16
Multiple Arrests, No
  Convictions
  (10b/c R) 49
My Brother's Leeper
  (7 R) 45
Nameless Arête
  (10c) ** 62
New Jersey Turnpike
  (V4 R) 54
New Testament
  (11a) ** 60
No Self Control (6 G) 64
Noncensus (9 R) 57
Noncensus Direct (10d) 57
Noncensus Redirect
  (12) 57
Nothing Yet (8 R) 57
Obnoxious Partner
  (5.8+ G) *** 66
Oh Promise Me (4 PG) 57
Old Chimney (1 G) 64
Open Face (5 R) 38

Open Face Slab
  (7- PG/R) 39
Orangutan (8 R) * 40
Orangutan Traverse
  (V3) ** 40
Orvie Direct
  (9+/10a TR) * 14
Outcast (9-) 44
Phone Booth
  (10a TR) *** 69
Practice Chimney
  (5 PG) 15
Practice Climb (2 G) * 15
Raising Cain (5.11a/b) 44
Rattlesnake (7 PG/R) * 36
Riff Raff Eliminate
  (10a PG/R) ** 37
Ripper Traverse
  (V2) ** 46
Ripper Up (V3) * 49
Ronca's Roof (8 R) 51
Route 1 (4 PG) 18
Route 2 (5/6 PG) 18
Run Out Of Favors
  (9+ R) 64
Shit Face (10b TR) 16
Short Face (V0-) 66
Slap (V2) * 51
Speechwriter Blues
  (7 PG) 54

Squatting Room Only
(6+ R) * 58

Stand and Deliver
(V5 R) 49

Super Slab (11a TR) 41

Technicolor (8 PG/R) 53

The Diamond
(10c TR) * 55

The End Climb (Orvie)
(8+ TR) ** 14

The Great Zawn
(Class 4) 42

The Hearth (5.8 PG/R) 58

The High Rocks Girdle
Traverse (10d) 70

The Last Stand
(9+ TR) * 70

The Long Chimney
(3 PG) * 39

The Low Traverse
(V5) ** 49

The Outsider (5.8) 44

The Problem (12a) ** 42

The Serpent (9+ R) 44

The Wizard Of Maz
(10d R) 44

Triple Overhang
(7 PG/R) * 15

Up (V1/V2) * 46

Up And Up (10d R) 46

Warmup Traverse
(V0+) * 16

Wham, Jam, Thank
You Cam (6 G/PG) 60

Zipperama (8 R) 64

CPSIA information can be obtained at www.ICGtesting.com
Printed in the USA
LVOW12s1049230114

370651LV00003B/836/P